Primary Sources of World Cultures™

CHINA

A PRIMARY SOURCE CULTURAL GUIDE

Gillian Houghton

The Rosen Publishing Group's
PowerPlus Books™
New York

Published in 2005 by The Rosen Publishing Group, Inc.
29 East 21st Street, New York, NY 10010

Copyright © 2005 by The Rosen Publishing Group, Inc.

First Edition

Library of Congress Cataloging-in-Publication Data

Houghton, Gillian.
China/Gillian Houghton.
    v. cm.—(Primary sources of world cultures) Includes bibliographical references and index. Audience: Ages 13–18.
Contents: The land—The people—The Chinese language—Chinese myths and legends—Chinese festivals and ceremonies of antiquity and today—The religions of China throughout its history—The art and architecture of China—The literature and music of China—Famous foods and recipes of China—Daily life and customs in China—Education and work in China.
ISBN 1-4042-2908-6 (library binding)
1. China—Juvenile literature. [1. China.] I. Title. II. Series.
DS706.H549 2005
951—dc22
2003027694

Manufactured in the United States of America

Cover images: Background: Text from the seventh-century sutra *Ten Kings of the World*. Center: The Great Wall of China. Bottom right: A young girl holds prayer sticks, which are used to tell fortunes.

Photo credits: cover (background), p. 38 © British Library, London, UK/Bridgeman Art Library; cover (middle), pp. 11, 66, 94, 100 (bottom), 118 (top inset) © Stone/Getty Images; cover (bottom), p. 57 © Steve McCurry/Magnum Photos; pp. 3, 118 (map), 120 © GeoAtlas; pp. 4 (top), 8 © Robb Kendrick/Aurora Photos; pp. 4 (middle), 16 (bottom) © Zuder/Laif/Aurora Photos; pp. 4 (bottom), 37, 87 © Michael Yamashita/IPN/Aurora Photos; pp. 5 (top), 5 (bottom), 50, 65, 75, 77 © Jodi Cobb/National Geographic Image Collection; pp. 5 (middle), 22 (bottom), 61 (top), 118 (bottom inset) © Cary Wolinsky/IPN/Aurora Photos; pp. 6, 7, 15, 54, 63 © Panorama Images/The Image Works; p. 9 © Dennis Cox/Age Fotostock; p. 10 (top) © Alvaro Leiva/Age Fotostock; p. 10 (bottom), 32, 74, 83, 115 © AFP/Getty Images; pp. 12, 36, 92 (top) © David McLain/Aurora Photos; p. 13 © Beth Wald/Aurora Photos; pp. 14, 16 (top), 52 © Hiroji Kubota/Magnum Photos; p. 17 (top) © Daniel A. Bedell/Animals Animals; p. 17 (bottom) © John Warden/SuperStock; pp. 18, 99 (top) © Michael Wolf/plus 49/The Image Works; pp. 19, 59, 82 (top) © Bettmann/Corbis; p. 20 © Erich Lessing/Art Resource, NY; pp. 21, 81 © The British Museum/Topham-HIP/The Image Works; p. 22 (top) © The British Library/Topham-HIP/The Image Works; p. 23 © Public Record Office/Topham-HIP/The Image Works; pp. 24, 26 (top) © Brown Brothers; pp. 25, 105 © Corbis; p. 26 (bottom), 27 (top) © Hulton/Archive/Getty Images; p. 27 (bottom), 106 (top) © AP/Wide World Photos; p. 28 © William Sewell/The Art Archive; p. 29 © Henri Cartier-Bresson/Magnum Photos; p. 30 © Topham/The Image Works; p. 31 © Private Collection/Bridgeman Art Library; p. 33 © Stuart Franklin/Magnum Photos; pp. 34, 84 © Patrick Zachmann/Magnum Photos; pp. 35, 49 © Ian Berry/Magnum Photos; pp. 39 (top), 90 © Giorgio Lotti/Contrasto/Redux; p. 39 (bottom) © Todd A. Gipstein/Corbis; p. 41 © Martin Peters/Image State; pp. 42, 85 © Mary Evans Picture Library; p. 43 © Robert Fried Photography; pp. 44, 104 © Bibliotheque Nationale, Paris, France/Bridgeman Art Library; p. 45 © Topkapi Palace Museum, Istanbul, Turkey/Bridgeman Art Library; p. 46 © Courtesy of the Library of Congress, Rare Book and Special Collections Division; p. 47 © 2003 Charles Walker/Topfoto/The Image Works; p. 48 © Oriental Museum, Durham University, UK/Bridgeman Art Library; p. 51 © Image State; pp. 53, 107 © Russell Gordon/Aurora Photos; pp. 55, 109 © Bob Sacha/IPN/Aurora Photos; p. 56 © Paolo Koch/Photo Researchers; p. 58 (top and bottom) © Werner Forman/Art Resource, NY; pp. 60 (top), 71 © National Palace Museum, Taipei, Taiwan/ Bridgeman Art Library; p. 60 (bottom) © Julia Waterlow/Eye Ubiquitous/Corbis; p. 61 (bottom) © Momatiuk Eastcott/The Image Works; p. 62 © Bridgeman Art Library; p. 64 © Chuck Nacke/IPN/Aurora Photos; pp. 67 (top), 70 © Asian Art & Archaeology, Inc./Corbis; p. 67 (bottom), 69 (top) © Réunion des Musées Nationaux/Art Resource, NY; p. 68 © Gift of Carol & Robert Straus/Museum of Fine Arts, Houston, Texas, USA/ Bridgeman Art Library; p. 69 (bottom), 91, 97, 111 © Michael Wolf/Aurora Photos; p. 71 (bottom) © David Noton/Image State; p. 72 © Ashmolean Museum, Oxford, UK/Bridgeman Art Library; p. 73 © Scala/Art Resource, NY; p. 76 © Alessandro D'Urso/Contrasto/Redux; p. 78 © British Museum, London, UK/Bridgeman Art Library; pp. 79, 80, 101 © Matton Images; p. 82 (bottom) © Lu Xun Memorial, Shanghai/The Huntington Archive of Buddhist and Related Art/The Ohio State University; p. 86 © Eric Sander/Cosmos/Aurora Photos; p. 89 © Dave Houser/Image State; pp. 92 (bottom), 99 (bottom) © Bruno Barbey/Magnum Photos; p. 93 © Photodisc Green/Getty Images; p. 95 © Laif/Aurora Photos; p. 96 © Masauki Suzuki/HAGA/The Image Works; p. 98 © Corbis Sygma; p. 100 (top) © Sean Sprague/The Image Works; p. 102 © SuperStock; p. 103 © National Museum, Seoul, Korea/Bridgeman Art Library; p. 106 (bottom) © Wally McNamee/Corbis; p. 110 © Chuck Fishman - Woodfin Camp/IPN/Aurora Photos; p. 113 © Peter Turnley/Corbis; p. 121 © Christoph Becker/Naturepl.com.

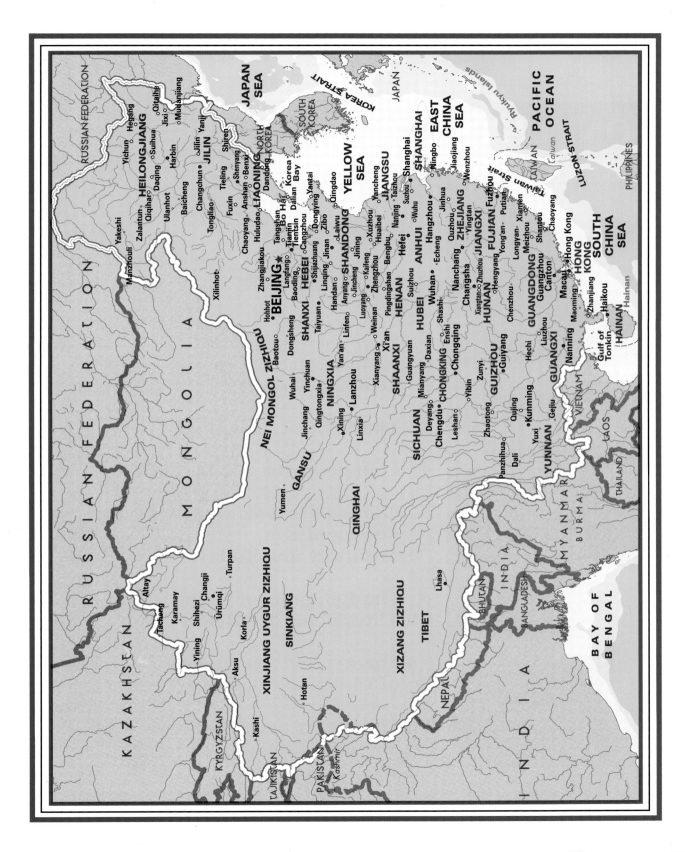

CONTENTS

INTRODUCTION

Among its ancient inhabitants, China was known as *Zhonghua*—the Middle or Central Kingdom—and as *Tianxia*, which translates to "everything under heaven." These names indicate the belief among the ancient Chinese that their country was the birthplace of civilization and the center of cultural development. This pride in China's long and rich history remains strong today, and for good reason. China boasts the most enduring civilization in the world. Written records of its existence date from nearly 4,000 years ago. By the third century BC, the Chinese had embraced Con-

fucianism, the teachings of the fifth-century BC Chinese philosopher Confucius and his followers. Confucianism provided the foundation for a wide range of political, social, and cultural institutions that survive to this day.

China's history has been marked by alternating cycles of great change, the return to more traditional ways, and promised reforms to society and government. The leaders of each age of the country's history have promised to renew a worn-out or corrupt political or social system. During

the imperial age, when powerful emperors governed the nation, each dynasty came to power on a wave of promised reforms that were deeply indebted to the

At left is a bamboo forest in Changning, Sichuan, in southwestern China. Known as the home of bamboo shoots, Changning produces more than 22 million pounds (10 million kilograms) of bamboo shoots per year. Bamboo is used to make furniture and other goods because of both its sturdiness and its ability to be bent and shaped. Above, Miao women adorn themselves in traditional garments and headdresses. With a population of from 7 to 8 million, the Miao are the fourth largest ethnic group in China and inhabit the southern mountainous regions of the country. Miao villages are composed of a few families and are scattered on mountain slopes and plains.

A farmer surveys his rice paddies. Rice paddies are shallow ponds where rice is grown. The paddies serve many purposes. They supply a wet place that is ideal for growing rice and attract several birds that prey on the insects that are harmful to rice plants.

traditions of the past. The Nationalist revolution of 1911 swept the country clean of an outdated and inefficient monarchy, replacing it with what was promised to be a modern republic (in which a president or prime minister was the head of state, rather than a king or an emperor).

With the Communist revolution of 1949, the Nationalist leaders were ousted, and China was again thrown into a period of radical change. This time, an unprecedented transformation of society and government—one marked by powerful successes and crippling failures—was begun. Although China developed into a strong military power and influential world player under Communism, its people often suffered poverty and repression and did not enjoy the same technological advances of Western nations.

In the 1970s, with the decline and death of Mao Zedong, China's longtime Communist leader, China again entered a new era of reform in which its economic, social, and cultural institutions came under the influence of the West. Yet if even

A cormorant fisherman holds a lantern to the water in order to lure the fish to the surface. A cormorant is a type of bird that dives into the water to hunt its prey. For nearly 1,000 years, Chinese fishermen have trained cormorants to catch fish, eels, and squid. Although it is no longer economical to use cormorants as a primary method of fishing, it is still a time-honored tradition and has become a popular tourist activity.

these reforms can be seen as the first steps on the road to democracy, then China is still far from its destination. Chinese citizens still experience a basic lack of freedom. The late 1980s and early 1990s saw large popular uprisings. These attempts at popular reform, illustrated most dramatically for a world audience by the 1989 student demonstrations in Beijing's Tian'anmen Square, were often violently suppressed. China's future is uncertain. What shape the next reform will take and when, if it develops at all, is not known.

Throughout its long history, China has appeared to outsiders as remote, isolated, and difficult to enter fully into and comprehend. It is surrounded by mountains, deserts, jungles, and ocean, which, for many centuries, isolated it from neighboring countries. The Chinese language is written in characters called ideograms. Ideograms are symbols that represent a thing or an idea, making it a very difficult language for Westerners to learn. Chinese is spoken in tones unfamiliar to Westerners

Several cyclists crowd Tian'anmen Square in the center of Beijing. It is said to be the biggest square in the world, able to hold 1 million people. The word *Tian'anmen* means the gate of heavenly peace. This gate is located on the north side of the square. Built in 1417, Tian'anmen Square has been the location for many revolts and political protests.

and difficult for nonnative Chinese speakers to imitate.

Cultural differences create another barrier to understanding China. An American tourist will encounter countless everyday customs that seem entirely foreign to him or her, beginning with simple details, such as the way a person is referred to by name. In China, an individual's surname (or family name) is said first, and his or her given name comes second. Hence, Mao Zedong is known as Chairman Mao, not Chairman Zedong.

Perhaps because of these differences, China is a fascinating country to study. However, Chinese culture is not simply the opposite of everything Western. In the literature and music of China, we find the universal themes of love, work, loyalty,

China's often harsh weather has wreaked havoc throughout the nation's long history. At left, disaster-relief workers search for survivors in the rubble left in the wake of Typhoon Durian in July 2001. In addition to loss of life, the storm caused more than $500 million worth of damage.

betrayal, humor, and tragedy. Chinese philosophers have posed the same questions about life, death, and the physical and spiritual worlds that have preoccupied Western thinkers for many centuries. In China's political and social history, we can recognize the familiar struggle between tradition and change that concerns all civilizations and societies, including our own.

Let's begin our exploration of China, a country of the new and the old, the familiar and the unexpected.

In southwestern China, a Hani riding a buffalo looks out over the rice fields. The Hani are one of China's many ethnic groups. In 1949, the Hani were liberated from the service of rich landowners. To repay the Hani for years of forced labor, the state gave the Hanis a large amount of farmland in the southern Yunnan Province. Being subtropical, the land is fertile and the rainfall plentiful—ideal for growing rice, millet, cotton, peanuts, indigo, and tea.

THE LAND

The Geography, Climate, and Wildlife of China

China is a vast country, extending roughly 3,000 miles (4,828 kilometers) from the independent republics of the former Soviet Union in the west to the Pacific Ocean in the east, and around 2,000 miles (3,219 km) from Russia in the north to Myanmar, Laos, and Vietnam in the south. The country's topography varies widely, from the snowy peaks of the Himalayas to the plains of the northeast. China's climate is equally varied and includes the bitter cold of Siberia, the tropical heat of Southeast Asia, the dry desert air of the Eurasian plateaus, and the wet, monsoonal weather of the South China Sea. About half of the area of the country—and nearly all of China's population—experiences two monsoons each year. The winter monsoon, a dry, cold storm that pushes south from Siberia and Mongolia, brings bitterly cold temperatures but little precipitation. In the summer, a wet monsoon originating over the South China Sea brings almost continual heavy showers to the southeastern provinces.

Politically, China is divided into twenty-three provinces (similar to states), five autonomous (or self-governing) ethnic regions, and four municipalities. The five autonomous regions of Tibet (Xizang), Xinjiang, Inner Mongolia (Nei Mongol), Guangxi, and Ningxia are given some freedom to govern themselves in acknowledgment of the cultural differences that exist between their residents and the majority of Chinese. The

At left, a hiker makes his way up the Mingsha Shan sand dunes located on the outskirts of Dunhuang. Dunhuang is an ancient small town near a junction of the Silk Road, a major trade route between the East and the West. Above, a train of yaks (long-haired oxen) are led across a Tibetan plateau toward Cho Oyu Mountain, part of the Himalayan range between the Tibet and Nepal border. Cho Oyu is the sixth tallest peak in the world, soaring 26,906 feet (8,201 m) into the sky.

Huang He, the Yellow River, is the second longest river in China, stretching more than 3,395 miles (5,464 km). Its source is in Qinghai Province in western China, and it empties into the Bohai Sea in Shandong Province after flowing through nine provinces, autonomous regions, and municipalities. It has the highest sand content of any river in the world. Every year, about 1.6 billion tons of sand stream into the Yellow River channels following floods. This sand gives the water its yellow color.

four municipalities, Beijing, Shanghai, Chongqing, and Tianjin, are cities that cover large urban and rural areas and have the status of provinces. In addition, Hong Kong, a British colony for much of the twentieth century, was returned to China in 1997. It is considered a "special administrative region."

Together, the provinces, municipalities, and autonomous regions, comprise China's mainland core, sometimes referred to as China proper.

The Mainland Core

The mainland core can be further divided into several geographic areas: northern, central, and southern China. Northern China encompasses the Huang He, or Yellow River, basin. The 3,395-mile (5,464-km) Yellow River begins in the mountain gorges of Qinghai Province and steers north, meandering in wide bends through the northern plains. For most of its

The Xizhimen overpass, a complex network of highways and an important subway, light rail, and train hub, is evidence of Beijing's rapid growth as a modern city. The overpass was built as part of Beijing's attempts to create a high-speed transportation system to carry people into, out of, and throughout Beijing quickly and efficiently.

course, it is a slow, shallow river that carries more than 1 billion tons of sediment to the Yellow Sea each year. The sediment, a rich soil called *loess*, comes from the Loess Plateau, which is eroded by the river's slow current. The soil's golden color gives the river its name. Much of the sediment is deposited on the riverbed farther downstream. As a result, the riverbed often rises to heights of between 10 and 40 feet (3 and 12 m) over the surrounding plain.

Throughout history, the Yellow River has seen countless cycles of drought and flood, earning it the nineteenth-century nickname China's Sorrow. Dams and dikes, or human-made walls, have been constructed to control the river's flow. Some of these projects were designed to prevent flooding or to provide water to farmers through irrigation, while others tried to make the river navigable to larger ships. Attempts to control and harness the Yellow River's power have had only limited success, however.

Northern China has long been known as the birthplace of Chinese civilization, and today it is the headquarters of the country's capital, Beijing. Beijing is at roughly the same latitude as Washington, D.C., but the Chinese capital experiences far greater extremes of climate. The winter monsoon sends temperatures plummeting below freezing, while the summer becomes extremely hot and dry. Because the summer monsoon originating in the South China Sea usually releases its downpours before reaching the north, the area averages only 20 to 25 inches (51 to 64 centimeters) of precipitation per year. So the people of northern China struggle through bitter cold winters and dry, hot summers. As a result, the growing season is short. The most successful crops are plants that thrive in drier climates, such as wheat, millet, and various legumes (such as beans).

A Chinese man beholds the beauty of yellow rape flowers in Jiangnan, south of the Yantgtze River in southeastern China. Rape flowers bloom in the springtime. Their seeds spread easily, which allows them to grow over miles of fields.

The provinces of central China are watered by the Chang Jiang, or Long River. In the West, it is more commonly known as the Yangtze River. The Yangtze River is 3,500 miles (5,633 km) long, making it the third-longest river in the world. As in the case of the Yellow River, the Yangtze has its source in the mountains of Qinghai Province. Unlike the Yellow River, however, the Yangtze runs swiftly eastward, through the country's most fertile agricultural land, to the province of Jiangsu, where it empties into the East China Sea. The Yangtze, connected to much of central China by a maze of tributaries (smaller streams that feed into a river), is an important transportation route.

The Yangtze River is critical to China's agricultural economy, but it also brings the occasional tragedy in the form of deadly floods. The wet summer monsoon contributes to an average yearly rainfall of roughly 40 inches (102 cm) across central China. As a result, the region enjoys a more varied agricultural economy and a longer growing season than does the north. Wheat, tea, and rice are planted in central China.

Modern skyscrapers rise above the city of Shanghai, in the central-eastern part of China, on the East China Sea. Shanghai is a large, bustling city filled with shops, restaurants, hotels, and high-rise apartment buildings.

In ancient China, pandas were believed to be magical creatures that had the ability to ward off evil spirits and natural disasters. Emperors prized their fur as a symbol of wealth.

Much of southern China is watered by the tributaries of Zhu Jiang, or the Pearl River. The largest of these tributaries is Xi Jiang, the West River. The West River, from its source in the Yunnan-Guizhou Plateau to its mouth in the city of Guangzhou (once known as Canton), flows for some 1,200 miles (1,931 km). Every summer, hurricanes beat the southern China coast, bringing the country's highest annual rainfalls. This wet climate is ideal for growing rice. Since the growing season often stretches for the full twelve months of the year, up to three harvests are collected each year.

Wildlife

China contains one of the world's largest number of wildlife species. Within its borders are 1,189 species of birds, 500 mammals, 210 amphibians, 320 reptiles, and 2,300 fish. Animals native only to China include the giant panda, golden monkey, white-lipped deer, Chinese alligator, brown-eared pheasant, and Chinese river dolphin. In the nation's 574 forest and wildlife nature reserves, China tries to protect almost 100 endangered species, including the panda, crested ibis (a water bird, one of the rarest in the world), black-necked crane, red-crowned crane, Asiatic elephant, snow leopard, South China tiger, and takin (similar to a musk ox).

The Corbett's tiger at right is also known as the Indo-Chinese tiger. The Indo-Chinese tiger is an endangered species and one of the few remaining tiger subspecies in Asia. Only about 1,200 Indo-Chinese tigers remain in existence.

THE PEOPLE

From the Imperial Age to the People's Republic of China

Some anthropologists and historians believe that the first Chinese migrated from Africa, the Middle East, central Asia, or India. Others argue, however, that the Chinese evolved independently on the northern plains of China, and the archaeological evidence largely supports this theory. In 1965, the remains of an early Pleistocene *Homo erectus*, a primitive ancestor of modern man dating from some 1.7 million years ago, were unearthed in southwestern China. Evidence of a more evolved middle-Pleistocene *Homo erectus*, one who walked upright and had a significantly larger brain than earlier fossils, was found southwest of Beijing in 1927 in the form of *Sinanthropus pekinensis*, known as Peking Man. The Peking Man lived about 500,000 years ago.

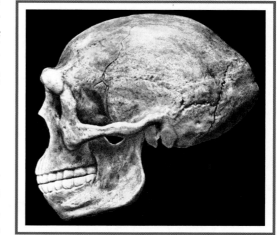

China in the Stone Age

Archaeological excavations have also unearthed a variety of Paleolithic, or Old Stone Age, artifacts that offer glimpses of life in China more than 20,000 years ago. According to this evidence, the northern plains enjoyed a mild climate. The Paleolithic man hunted rhinoceroses, antelope, ostriches, and bison. He had discovered

At left, workers clean a statue of Mao Zedong in Chengdu, China. Mao Zedong founded and led the People's Republic of China from 1949 until his death in 1976. Under his leadership, China was unified and declared itself an independent, self-governing country after a long period of foreign domination, civil war, and revolution. Above is the reconstructed skull of Peking Man, a *Homo erectus* (an early species that preceded modern man) who lived from 300,000 to 600,000 years ago near what is now Beijing.

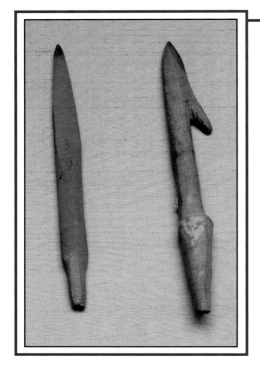

These Neolithic tools from c. 3000 BC were most likely used for fishing and hunting. They were excavated at Wu-Chiang in Kiang-Shu, China, and are currently on display at the National Museum in Beijing. During the Neolithic period, people used tools of stone. The Bronze Age began in c. 2000 BC when people began working with metals.

how to control and use fire for warmth and cooking and had made a few simple tools out of animal bone.

With the advance of the glaciers across the Asian continent at the end of the Paleolithic period came dramatic climate change. Temperatures dropped and great winds blew. These environmental changes might have driven many of China's residents across the Bering Strait to North America, where they gave rise to the first Inuit and Native American peoples. Meanwhile, China remained virtually uninhabited throughout the Mesolithic period or Middle Stone Age.

Evidence of human settlement would not reappear until the Neolithic period, or New Stone Age, by which time the Chinese engaged in settled agricultural activities, like planting crops and raising animals. The earlier nomadic existence of hunting and gathering was a thing of the past. The Chinese broke the soil with stone-bladed hoes and planted vegetables and grains. They raised pigs, dogs, sheep, and cattle. Primitive bone tools gave way to stone knives, bows and arrows, and woven baskets. The people lived in villages that could be defended against enemies and wore clothes of animal skin or woven cloth made from hemp.

The Dawn of the Imperial Era

The Shang, later known as the Yin, is the first dynasty whose existence is supported by archaeological evidence. A wealth of ceremonial artifacts (used primarily for divination, or future-predicting rites) survives from the period, as well as examples of Shang-era pottery and bronze weapons and tools. Nobles lived in large, spacious palaces made of pounded earth and brick and covered by gabled roofs. The general population, however, lived in Neolithic-era dugouts, cave dwellings, or thatched huts. Life for the common

This Shang dynasty jade ring was made sometime between 1500 and 1050 BC and inscribed with poetic inscriptions. The ring once belonged to Emperor Qianlong of the Qing dynasty, who ruled China from 1735 to 1796.

Chinese under Shang rule was filled with backbreaking agricultural labor and little else.

The Shang was followed by the Zhou dynasty. With the victory of the Qin and its first ruler, Qin Shi Huangdi, over the Zhou in 221 BC, the imperial era began. Shi Huangdi unified China's various warring states and nomadic peoples under a strong, centralized government led by an all-powerful emperor, namely himself. The emperor was believed to have a mandate from heaven, meaning that he was heaven's representative on Earth and therefore not to be opposed.

After the emperor's death in 210 BC, the Qin dynasty came to an end. Various regional groups struggled to fill the power void. From the dust of battle rose Liu Pang, a man of humble beginnings. In 202 BC, having defeated his competitors, Liu established the Han dynasty. With only a brief interruption, from AD 9 to AD 23, the Han dynasty would rule China for some 400 years.

The Han Dynasty

Liu Pang and his Han successors were smart and skillful rulers. Under the Han dynasty, the Chinese enjoyed a period of unprecedented political, intellectual, creative, and economic development. The accomplishments of the Han dynasty were long lasting and far-reaching. In recognition of this period of great productivity and social and political stability, the Chinese call themselves the Han race, and the core provinces of mainland China are known as Han China.

Political principles that were first introduced by Emperor Shi Huangdi of the Qin dynasty, including the notion of a heaven-sent emperor and the system of civil service exams (see chapter 11), were adopted and expanded under the Han dynasty, taking

At left is a portrait of Qin Shi Huangdi, China's first emperor. He was said to have greatly feared death and sent out a party to hunt for a pill that would make him immortal. Instead, his party settled in Japan.

firm root in the minds of the Chinese people. The philosophy of Confucius, which stressed the importance of imperial order and bureaucratic rule, became the state's official philosophy and the foundation of scholarship at the new imperial university.

Under Han emperors, China's borders extended south to Vietnam, north to Manchuria and northern Korea, and west to the Caspian Sea. Port records indicate a thriving international trade as well. China imported wool, linen, ivory, and horses. It exported silk along the vast silk routes that wound westward through the plateaus and deserts, spreading Chinese economic and cultural influence to the country's distant neighbors. Accounts dating from AD 57 describe the first known diplomatic mission from Japan, received by the Han emperor in Luoyang, which was then the capital city.

In the second century AD, the increasingly corrupt Han dynasty collapsed under the pressure of various rebellions. What followed were 350 years of conflict known as the Six Dynasties, or Liu Chao. After the period of the Six Dynasties ended, the short-lived Sui rose and fell, followed by the more enduring Tang dynasty.

Bezeklik is a Buddhist retreat near the Gobi Desert, along the 4,000 mile-long (6,437-km long) Silk Road. The city was carved out of thickly packed dust called loess sometime during the seventh century AD. The interior walls of Bezeklik are decorated with both Christian and Buddhist religious paintings.

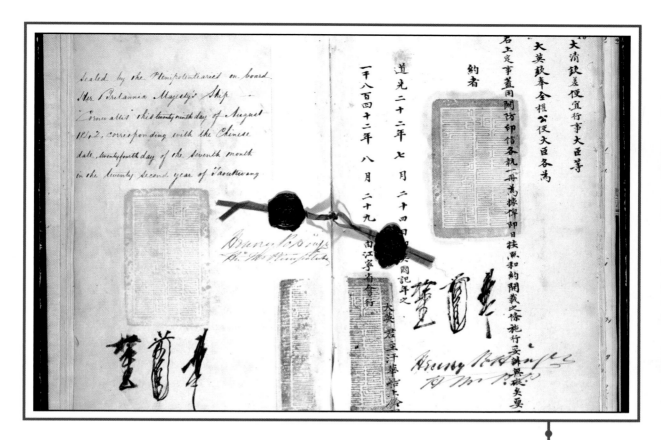

Another period of conflict and disunity, known as the Five Dynasties, followed. Imperial unity was then reasserted by the Song dynasty, followed by the Yüan, Ming, and Qing (or Manchu) dynasties.

The Coming of the West

Under the Qing (or Manchu) dynasty, China became the largest and wealthiest country in the world. Its borders reached into Mongolia, central Asia, Taiwan, and Tibet. New food crops, such as sweet potato, corn, and sorghum (a tropical grass similar to Indian corn), along with an ever-greater proportion of cash crops, such as tobacco, tea, and cotton, helped feed the Chinese. They also provided the people with valuable agricultural products to export, spurring regional and international trade.

International trade also grew in response to increased foreign demand for Chinese goods such as porcelain and lacquerware (wooden objects such as bowls, plates, and

The Nanking Treaty *(above)* ended the three-year-long Opium War between China and Britain over the British practice of importing opium from India and selling it to Chinese addicts. The treaty was signed on August 29, 1842, and allowed the British to continue selling opium in China.

cups coated with a thick, shiny varnish). Chinese merchants began setting up shop in foreign port cities. With increased trade came new, alarming threats, however—population growth and the influence of the Western world. In Europe and the United States, the Industrial Revolution was about to transform society, boost the economy, and increase the standard of living. Europe, the United States, and Japan (which was also benefiting from modernization) began to look beyond their borders in search of raw materials and markets for their manufactured goods. For many years, the British East India Company had made a handsome profit by sending opium—a powerful drug—to China from India, which was then a British colony. The Chinese government outlawed the trade, but opium continued to pour into China, creating a nation of addicts who wasted much of their money on the drug.

When Chinese authorities seized and burned cargoes of British opium in 1840, war between the two nations broke out. The Opium War ended in 1842 with the Treaty of Nanjing, which gave Hong Kong to the British crown. This agreement opened the ports of Guangzhou, Shanghai, Ningbo, Fuzhou, and Xiamen to unrestricted British trade and settlement. In addition, the Qing government was forced to pay a fine to the British government. In later treaties, the Chinese were forced to give up even more political and economic autonomy.

This loss of independence inspired China's self-strengthening movement, which sought to create a strong and self-sufficient China that could live independently of foreign money and interference. The conservative members of the imperial family, presided over by Empress Dowager Cixi (1835– 1908), chose to defend China by allying themselves with the Boxers United in Righteousness, a fanatical group

Chinese citizens, unhappy with foreign influence and opposed to the Manchu Qing ruling dynasty, adopted the slogan "Overthrow the King. Destroy the foreigner." These nineteenth-century rebels, known as Boxers, were part of a revolutionary group called the Fists of Righteous Harmony.

Two accused members of the Boxer Rebellion kneel before the Chinese High Court. After the unsuccessful rebellion, ten people believed to be ringleaders were executed.

of peasants. The Boxers practiced martial arts and claimed to be immune to attacks by any human weapon thanks to the protection of mass spirit possession. Originating in the poor agriculture-based province of Shandong, the Boxers spread north, physically attacking Christian missionaries, Chinese who had converted to Christianity, and any example of the foreign presence in China, including churches and railway lines.

In August 1900, a foreign force of some 20,000 soldiers entered Beijing and ended the rebellion. The previous day, the imperial court had fled the city. By order of the Boxer Protocol of 1901, Chinese officials who had supported the Boxer Rebellion were executed or exiled and Chinese diplomatic missions were sent abroad to apologize for the murders of missionaries and diplomats. Foreign armies were allowed to gather significant reinforcements along the east coast near Beijing. Finally, the Qing government was ordered to pay a fine of $333 million, to be divided among the foreign powers affected by the rebellion.

The Boxer Rebellion left the Qing dynasty penniless and even weaker than before. The Qing dynasty and the entire dynastic system soon came to a bitter end.

The Nationalists and Communists

During World War I (1914–1918) Japan invaded China. Even after the war's end, Japan was allowed to control several parts of China. In response to this, the

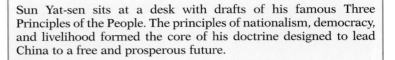

Sun Yat-sen sits at a desk with drafts of his famous Three Principles of the People. The principles of nationalism, democracy, and livelihood formed the core of his doctrine designed to lead China to a free and prosperous future.

Guomindang (the Nationalist Party that was founded by Sun Yat-sen and had overthrown imperial rule) and the Chinese Communist Party joined forces as the United Front, bound by an anti-imperialist philosophy. The following year, Sun Yat-sen died. His leadership role in Guomindang was soon filled by an experienced military commander named Chiang Kai-shek. Chiang tried to gain control of the party by ridding it of Communists. In Shanghai, Chiang abolished trade unions and executed known Communists and their supporters.

In 1936, the Guomindang and the Chinese Communist Party—led by Mao Zedong, a former library assistant at Beijing University—buried their differences and joined forces once again, this time to drive Japanese troops out of Manchuria and northern China. In July 1937, the united Chinese forces met Japanese troops near Beijing, sparking the beginning of the Second Sino-Japanese War (the first, a struggle over control of Korea, occurred in the late nineteenth century). Before long, Japan had captured several major cities, and Chiang Kai-shek was forced to relocate the Nationalist government to the western city of Chongqing.

The conflict between China and Japan dragged on for several more years and merged with the

A former aide to Sun Yat-sen, Chiang Kai-shek helped to overthrow the Qing dynasty and establish a Nationalist government in its place. After rising to the leadership of the Nationalists, he lost the civil war with the Communists and was forced to move his government to Taipei, Taiwan, in 1950. There he established the Republic of China.

The People: From the Imperial Age to the People's Republic of China

Born to peasants, Mao Zedong, seen at right in 1925, was trained in Chinese classics and then received a modern education. After observing China's oppressive social conditions, he became one of the first members of China's Communist Party.

Western Allies' battles against Japan during World War II (1939–1945). With the American atomic bomb attack on the Japanese cities of Hiroshima and Nagasaki, however, World War II came to a sudden end.

Though both the Chinese Communist Party and the Guomindang were weakened by eight years of fighting the Japanese, the bitter struggle between the two parties began again right where it had left off before the war. Chiang's troops were now larger and better equipped, but Mao's soldiers were better led and inspired. In April 1949, Mao's forces, which had been renamed the People's Liberation Army, crossed the Yangtze River and prepared to conquer southern China. In October, Mao stood at the entrance to the Forbidden City (the former palace of China's emperor) in Beijing and announced the creation of the People's Republic of China. In the following months, Chiang and the Guomindang retreated to Taiwan, where they established what they said was the true government of the Republic of China.

Japanese soldiers run into battle during the Second Sino-Japanese War in July 1937. The following December, the Japanese took over Nanjing, then the capital city of China, and brutally killed more than 250,000 Chinese civilians in what became known as the Nanjing Massacre.

The Birth of Communist China

Almost immediately after the formation of the People's Republic of China, the Chinese Communist Party embarked on a nationwide program of land reform, the cornerstone of the Communist agenda. Between 1949 and 1952, property was seized from landlords—who made up just 4 percent of the population but owned 30 percent of the land—and redistributed to peasants.

The next step in Mao's plan, announced in 1955, was the collectivization of land into APCs, or agricultural producers' cooperatives. This meant that from then on, peasants would come together, give up individual control and private ownership of their land, and form mutual aid groups. The fruits of their labor—crops, produce, dairy products, and livestock—and the money they earned would be held collectively and distributed among all the members of the work unit equally. Marriage reforms, bureaucratic reorganization, the loss of private property, and the gradual nationalization (public, or government, ownership) of all private enterprises were also undertaken.

The Great Leap Forward

In 1958, the Chinese Communist Party launched a new program called the Great Leap Forward, aimed at realizing Mao's vision of a rapid industrialization that would usher China and its workers into a modern paradise. The foundation of this movement was the commune, a group of APCs that would work together for the good of the community and the entire nation.

The commune oversaw the social, political, and economic life of its members. Communes recruited local militias and organized schools and rural health clinics. A commune's members were required to eat meals in a communal dining hall. Their personal belongings were confiscated and shared among other members. When

The 1949 poster at left reads "People from the Rivers and Mountains." Many propaganda posters similar to this one were used throughout Mao's career to promote his policies. This poster celebrates his defeat of the Nationalists and the founding of the People's Republic of China. Above, members of the commune of Shiu Shin walk in file toward the commune's dining hall. The Shiu Shin commune was composed of 280 villages and was home to 310,000 inhabitants.

ordered by the government, they were required to abandon their agricultural chores to work on public projects. Increasingly, this resulted in food shortages.

The enforcement of these measures and the resulting lack of personal freedom often met with popular unrest. In December 1958, Mao Zedong announced his intention to step down as president of the People's Republic. In April 1959, he would be replaced by Liu Shaoqi. Over the next two years, northern China faced a relentless drought, while southern China was battered by floods. Agricultural production fell, and famine spread across the country. Between 1959 and 1961, some 30 million Chinese died. The Great Leap Forward, widely criticized in China and abroad, came to an official end in 1960. A retreat from Mao's agricultural policies was led by Liu Shaoqi and another important Communist Party official, Deng Xiaoping.

The Cultural Revolution

Mao Zedong did not make a humble exit from the political scene, however. He continued to speak out, promoting socialist ideals and condemning what he called "revisionism"—backsliding into the "evils" of capitalism. His efforts, however, were met with little enthusiasm in the party, and his programs went nowhere.

Mao decided to wage an all-out campaign against the party leadership, a campaign that would come to be known as the Great Proletarian Cultural Revolution. In early 1966, Mao forced the dismissal of several high-ranking party officials. He publicly called for revolt against all forms of authority. The first people to hear his battle cry were students at Beijing University, who were soon marching in protest and speaking out against teachers, intellectuals, and government officials. These demonstrations sparked the creation of the Red

Members of the Red Guard and other revolutionaries joyfully hang pro-socialist posters on the walls of a university during Mao's Cultural Revolution. Though the Cultural Revolution turned out to be a bloody failure, many Chinese—particularly the young—were initially inspired and excited by Mao's strongly anticapitalist, anti-Western stance.

This Cultural Revolution-era propaganda poster is entitled "Reporting Our Harvest to Chairman Mao." Such posters were designed to glorify life on the communes, which in reality was often harsh and marked by poverty and hunger.

Guards—organized groups of high school and college-age activists who entered the struggle for Maoist China.

In July 1966, Mao called a party conference, at which he announced the aims of the Cultural Revolution. He reiterated his criticism of "revisionists" and added to the agenda the destruction of the "four olds"—old ideas, old habits, old culture, and old customs. After demoting or expelling those who opposed him within the party, Mao encouraged the Red Guards to tour the country, spreading revolutionary spirit and attacking any symbol of tradition and authority: libraries, temples, public officials, classical musicians, teachers, and their homes. Even harmless hobbies, such as fishing, keeping pets, and planting gardens, were condemned.

His admirers, numbering around 14 million, followed orders, and violence broke out across the country to a degree and intensity unexpected even by Mao. The movement soon spiraled out of control. In September 1967, Mao was forced to order the People's Liberation Army to subdue the Red Guard. Thousands of student revolutionaries were killed, while others were sent to the countryside for "re-education." While the Cultural Revolution ended in 1969, Mao's repressive influence continued until his death in 1976.

The End of Maoist China

Mao was succeeded by the party's first vice chairman, Hua Guofeng, who continued to praise the accomplishments of the Cultural Revolution. It was not until Deng Xiaoping's return to power in 1977 that a new and less repressive era began.

Under Deng, the commune system disintegrated. By 1983, nearly all peasant households operated under the "household responsibility" system, by which individuals

Chinese leader Deng Xiaoping *(left)* dominated both the Communist Party and China's government throughout the 1980s, instituting a variety of economic reforms aimed at opening the country to international trade and free markets. He resigned from his last party post in 1989, after supporting the use of military force against Tian'anmen Square protesters. Deng died in 1997 after nine years in office.

could lease land from the collectives and manage the land themselves. A certain percentage of their harvest would be owed to the state, and the rest could be sold in a free market (where prices are not kept artificially low by the government). In the cities, the government also loosened its grip on industry, allowing privately owned businesses to open, state-run businesses to operate more independently, and foreign companies to invest in Chinese businesses.

These economic reforms dramatically changed the lifestyle and increased the living standard of average Chinese, but they were not accompanied by any political reforms. The Chinese continued to suffer under an oppressive government that severely limited their personal freedoms. Unrest began to grow again.

Student Demonstrations and the Tian'anmen Square Massacre

In December 1986, student protesters demanded the right to free speech, a free press, and a limited form of democracy in which politicians would have to be more responsive to the citizens they represented. The movement soon fizzled, but the civil unrest that lay beneath it continued to simmer. In rural areas, decollectivization—the return of communally held land to individuals—had led to a widening gap between rich and poor people. Disagreements between neighbors and between neighboring villages over natural resources such as farmland and water sources began to break out.

In the cities, state-sector employees, including teachers, bureaucrats, and industrial workers, were also growing more angry. Their fixed salaries did not increase with the cost of living in an increasingly free-market economy.

Government-employed urban workers soon went on strike. Meanwhile, students began protesting against Japanese economic influence, atomic weapons tests, the presence of foreign university students, corruption within the Chinese Communist Party, and many other social concerns.

In April 1989, Communist Party chairman Hu Yaobang died. Thousands of mourners gathered in Beijing's Tian'anmen Square to honor him. Student protesters, unmoved by his death, instead issued a petition demanding that the party investigate Hu, publish the salaries paid to top party officials

Tanks roll toward Tian'anmen Square to break up pro-democracy demonstrations in 1989. Approximately 1.5 million workers and students participated in the protests. The Chinese Red Cross estimates that approximately 2,600 civilians died in the military crackdown that followed six weeks of largely peaceful demonstrations.

and their families, institute a free press and the right to free expression, and increase the wages paid to university teachers. When their petition was rejected by party officials, the students began to organize protests.

On April 26, some 100,000 students marched into Tian'anmen Square. By May 4, the square was crowded with 150,000 students, and similar protests had begun in Shanghai, Changsha, Nanjing, and Wuhan. Between May 4 and May 19, an estimated 1.5 million students and university employees participated in the demonstrations

On May 18, 1989, leaders of the pro-democracy movement *(left)* met with government officials in hopes of finding a solution to the conflict and having some of their demands met. On June 4, however, the government ceased negotiations and ordered the People's Liberation Army to open fire on the Tian'anmen protesters, killing several thousand.

nationwide. When negotiations between students and party leaders reached a dead end, the Politburo, the policy-making executive committee of the Communist Party, declared martial law. Tanks rumbled through the streets of Beijing. Through the evening and early morning of June 3 and 4, more than 200,000 armed troops entered the square and began firing on protesters. Estimates of the dead and wounded vary greatly. Official Chinese records number the dead at 300, but unofficial accounts estimate that between 2,000 and 7,000 civilians died, mostly residents of Beijing killed by tanks on their way to Tian'anmen Square.

What followed were mass arrests and the official condemnation of the Tian'anmen Square protests as "counterrevolutionary." Many student leaders and outspoken intellectuals who avoided arrest were forced into exile in Europe and the United States. Communist Party leadership was assumed by Jiang Zemin, who, in 1993, became president. Jiang pursued a policy of economic development—based in large part on foreign investment and trade—and of political stability. China's growing willingness to open its country to foreign trade had the effect of quieting international outrage over the Tian'anmen Square massacre.

China Today

Today, China is a socialist market economy. This means that the usual capitalist law of supply and demand—in which prices and production are set only by the level of demand for the products—is regulated by the government to make sure prices do not get too high and workers remain busy. China's workers are represented by the

The bright lights and bustle of the Wan Chai district are the main draw for many travelers to Hong Kong. Hong Kong was occupied by Great Britain in 1841 and remained its colony until 1997, when it was given back to China. China has promised that its socialist economic system will not be imposed on Hong Kong's free markets and that Hong Kong will enjoy autonomy in all matters except foreign and defense affairs for the next fifty years.

elected members of the National People's Congress and the local people's congresses. The president serves as head of state, along with a vice president. The Chinese Communist Party remains the only political party in power. The other eight recognized political parties can express their views through political conferences and forums only at the invitation of the Communist Party.

There is still a great deal of social and political unrest in China, though opposition to the party is suppressed and student activism is virtually nonexistent. The economic reforms of the past decade have brought new challenges, including a rising crime rate. Ethnic unrest in the nation's outlying regions has received international attention. Official corruption has spread. Yet China's long history is not at an end. Though the call for democracy has been all but silenced, the country continues to grow and change. It seems likely that if the Communist Party hopes to survive far into the twenty-first century, it too will have to grow and change. Its ability to adapt to the nation's growing desire for personal and political freedom may also determine the survival of China as a whole.

THE CHINESE LANGUAGE

3

The Chinese written language is made up of characters known as ideograms. Each character represents an idea, and words can be made up of one or more characters. Thus, the word for school, transliterated as *xuexiao*, combines the character *xue*, which means "study," and the character *xiao*, which means "corral." At the same time, however, a complicated idea that would require many words of explanation in English can be expressed very simply in a single character.

Characters, of which there are some 50,000, are made of combinations of strokes. A single character may have up to twenty-eight strokes, drawn in a precise sequence and form. The slightest deviation from the usual order and direction of the strokes can alter the meaning of the character. A Chinese student who has achieved basic literacy—after many long hours of study and memorization—can comprehend around 3,000 characters. The average newspaper is written for the reader with a working knowledge of about 7,000 characters.

Some characters are simplified pictures of the objects they represent. For example, the character for "mouth" is a small square. Some characters are familiar

At left, intrigued bystanders watch a skillful calligrapher practice the ancient decorative writing that is considered one of the highest forms of Chinese art. The man is using water and a writing sponge attached to the end of a stick. There are many styles of writing calligraphy. They range from a very formal, traditional method that uses wide, steady brushstrokes, to thinner, more quick and fluid strokes. Perfection is not required or prized. In fact, ink blots or dry brushstrokes are thought to be more expressive and revealing of the artist's personality. Above, young Tajik boys do their homework before school starts. The Tajik are an ethnic minority in China, descended from Iranians who migrated to central Asia.

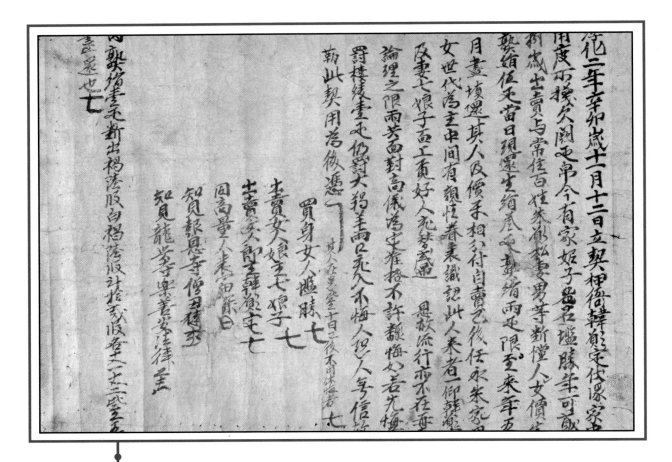

representations of abstract ideas. The characters for the numbers one, two, and three are each made by the appropriate number of straight lines. Finally, some characters are phonetic, in that they are made up of symbols that the reader would recognize as representing a particular sound.

Wén-yán and Bái-huà

The written language appears in two forms: classical, or *wén-yán*, and vernacular, or *bái-huà*. Wén-yán and bái-huà use the same characters, but each carries different connotations and meanings. Vernacular language is less formal and more like typical conversational language. It is the language of the average person. Classical Chinese was the language of the early Confucian texts and of the imperial-era civil service examinations. It was written without punctuation

A Beijing bookstore displays its wares. Because of its large and literate population, there is a huge demand for books in both urban and rural areas. Given China's 1 billion citizens and millions of Chinese speakers living throughout the world, it is estimated that one in five people on Earth speak Chinese.

and read in columns from top to bottom and from right to left across the page. In addition, the front of Chinese books are what Westerners would consider the back. It took many years of study to master wén-yán in preparation for the very demanding examinations that would determine one's career and social status. Following the May Fourth Movement of 1919, which emphasized Chinese nationalism and native traditions, bái-huà became the standard written language in China (see chapter 8).

Dialects

The written language is universal across China, but its pronunciation varies widely among local dialects. There are seven major dialects of Chinese, and they vary so dramatically that it is difficult for speakers of different dialects to understand one another.

A sign for an Internet café in Beijing is written in both English and Chinese. Because Chinese characters are extremely difficult for nonnative speakers to understand, many Chinese businesses that attract foreign customers will use and speak English.

Examples of Characters

英 Courage 命 Destiny 朋友 Friend

貴 Honor 愛 Love 月 Moon

平 Peace 孚 Truth 星 Star

Mandarin, as it is known by Westerners, is the most common dialect, spoken by about 70 percent of the population. In fact, Mandarin is spoken by more people than any other language in the world.

In 1955, the government decided that the variant of Mandarin spoken in Beijing would be the official national language, or *pûtônghuà*, which translates as "common speech." However, although tourists and traveling businesspeople might be well-advised to buy a Mandarin phrasebook, they will be unprepared to converse with the many millions of people who continue to speak one of the other prominent Chinese dialects. One of the most common of these is known as Cantonese. Cantonese is the primary dialect of Hong Kong and the province of Guangxi. Other dialects, including Mongolian, Manchurian, and Miao, are spoken in the outlying ethnic regions and to a lesser degree, in central China.

Mandarin is made up of about 420 syllables, or units of sound composed of a consonant and a vowel. However, each syllable can be spoken using four different tones: high, rising, falling-rising, and falling. This allows for nearly 1,700 distinct sounds. By comparison, English has about 1,200 different sounds. These tones create such subtle differences that the nonnative speaker may find it difficult to hear the variations of tone and virtually impossible to reproduce the various sounds. Each spoken character represents a single syllable, and each syllable is given a tone. The tone changes the sound of the syllable and thus the meaning of what is being said.

Language Reforms

The Chinese government has initiated reforms in the hopes of making it easier to learn how to read and write the language. In 1956, several hundred characters were redesigned in simpler forms. In 1958, the *pinyin* system of transliteration, which uses the twenty-six letters of the Latin, or Roman, alphabet, was instituted.

Despite these attempts to make Chinese more accessible to Westerners, there has not yet been any call to get rid of the system of characters altogether. Without continued familiarity with characters, Chinese people would lose a strong link to their past. Classic texts would become unreadable to anyone who did not learn characters. Cut off from their shared written language and using very different phonetic alphabets, speakers of different dialects would lose their ability to communicate with each other. The Chinese written language, though a challenging and difficult system to learn, is a central part of Chinese culture, both ancient and modern. It has long been a powerful medium through which stories are told, history is related, ideas are shared, and ideologies are championed.

CHINESE MYTHS AND LEGENDS

4

According to legend, Chinese civilization was born on the northern plains. This belief is largely supported by archaeological evidence, as we have seen (see chapter 2). For this reason, Chinese mythology, and the literary classics based on it, is generally confined to this geographic area.

Popular Chinese myths incorporate a powerful educational element. Each myth was created to teach its audience about the basic values shared by the culture, specifically the importance of family, of agriculture, and of the righteous king.

The Story of Pangu and the Origin of Chinese Civilization

Sometime in the fourth century AD, the Chinese began telling the story of Pangu (also known as Ban Gu or Pan Ku), the original being. Pangu spent 18,000 years carving the universe out of chaos. He organized the primordial (early and unformed) cosmos into the forces of *yin* and *yang*. Yin is associated with woman, with negative space, darkness, destruction, and passivity. Yang is associated with man, with positive space, light, construction, and activity. The symbol to represent yin and yang is a circle divided in two by a curved line. It is meant to

The painting at left depicts the Eight Immortals crossing the sea. It is inspired by an old Chinese fable that tells the story of how eight gods and goddesses each used their respective magic charms to help them get across the ocean. The moral of the story is that there is more than one way to accomplish a task. Above: A yin-yang symbol is set into the pavement of Old Town Square in Lijiang. The yin-yang symbol represents the balance of opposing forces in the universe. Yin represents darkness, the Moon, and femininity, and yang symbolizes light, the Sun, and masculinity.

represent an egg. The yolk, a dark circle on a light background, occupies the left or top half. The white of the egg, a light circle on a dark background, occupies the right or lower half. The idea of two complementary yet competing forces is central to Chinese thought. As we shall see, it plays a role in religion, medicine, and even food.

When Pangu died, scavenging creatures gathered and fed on his corpse. These creatures became the human race and gave rise to a long line of kings, each possessing superhuman abilities. Traditional Chinese accounts describe twelve brothers known as the celestial (heavenly) emperors, each half man and half serpent, who were empowered and directed by heaven to rule for 18,000 years. They were followed by the eleven terrestrial (earthly) emperors, another family of brothers that ruled for 18,000 years. Next came the nine human emperors, each of whom conquered one-ninth of the world. They would rule for 46,500 years. In total, these mythic emperors ruled for more than 80,000 years.

The succeeding sixteen mythic kings are known to modern historians only by their names. Next came the *huang*, or legendary monarchs, Fu Xi, Shen Nong, and Huang Di. Fu Xi is said to have ruled for more than 115 years, from 2852 BC to 2737 BC. According to Chinese myth, he is responsible for the domestication of animals; the invention of fishing, music, and writing; and important developments in early religious rites and ceremonies. He is also credited with inventing flood control, and, with his wife, Nu Wa, the institution of marriage. Shen Nong, who reigned from 2734 BC to 2697 BC, invented agriculture and medicine. Huang Di (2697–2597), also known as the Yellow Emperor, is perhaps the most famous legendary

A nineteenth-century color engraving depicts China's legendary huang monarchs *(from left to right)*, **Huang Di, Fu Xi,** and **Shen Nong.** Together they are called the inventors of Chinese civilization for their supposed contributions to farming, animal domestication, medicine, politics, law, and religion.

A hand-colored engraving by French artist Pierre Duflos shows the Sage King Yu. Throughout Chinese history the Sage Kings have been celebrated for their selfless dedication to the welfare of their people.

monarch in Chinese mythology. He is said to have invented the wheel, bricks, the lunar calendar, and the recording of history.

Next came the Sage Kings (also known as the Model Emperors), who did not inherit but earned their thrones through their merits as leaders. Yao, Shun, and Yu are credited with inventing a variety of tools without which Chinese civilization could not have grown and prospered. Shun invented the principle of weights and measures. Yu is credited with controlling and harnessing the waters of the Yellow River by building levees and canals. This engineering feat brought an end to the devastating seasonal floods along the river and made large-scale agriculture possible. Yu is also celebrated as the founder of the first traditional Chinese dynasty, the Xia.

The Zodiac and Gods of Daily Life

In the Chinese tradition, both the grand cycles of the universe and the everyday toils of humans are full of mythic significance, thanks to the zodiac. The zodiac is the group of twelve signs or constellations that represent a portion of the imaginary band that encircles the planets and their paths.

According to legend, an emperor invited all the animals of the world to a banquet. Only twelve animals came, and the emperor honored these twelve by naming the signs of the Chinese zodiac for them: rat, ox, tiger, rabbit, dragon, snake, horse, goat, monkey, rooster, dog, and pig. Each year is represented by one of these twelve creatures, also known as the Twelve Earthly Branches. People born during a certain year are believed to share the characteristics of the animal associated with that year. For example, people

Pangu and the Creation of the World

In the beginning, there was darkness everywhere, and chaos ruled. Within the darkness there formed an egg, and inside the egg the giant Pangu came into being. For eons, safely inside the egg, Pangu slept and grew. When he had grown to gigantic size, he stretched his huge limbs and in so doing broke the egg. The lighter parts of the egg floated upward to form the heavens, and the denser parts sank downward, to become Earth. And so was formed Earth and sky, yin and yang.

Pangu saw what had happened and he was pleased. But he feared that heaven and Earth might meld together again, so he placed himself between them, his head holding up the sky and his feet firmly upon Earth. Pangu continued to grow at a rate of ten feet a day for 18,000 years, so increasing the distance between heaven and Earth, until they seemed fixed and secure, 30,000 miles (42,280 km) apart. Now exhausted, Pangu went back to sleep and never woke up.

Pangu died, and his body went to make the world and all its elements. The wind and clouds were formed from his breath, his voice was thunder and lightning, his eyes became the Sun and the Moon, his arms and his legs became the four directions of the compass, and his trunk became the mountains. His flesh turned into the soil and the trees that grow on it, his blood into the rivers that flow, and his veins into paths men travel. His body hair became the grass and herbs, and his skin the same, and precious stones and minerals were formed from his bones and teeth. His sweat became the dew, and the hair of his head became the stars that trail throughout heaven. As for the parasites on his body, these became the diverse races of humankind.

Although Pangu is dead, some say he is still responsible for the weather, which fluctuates according to his moods.

From: Lin, Te. *Teach Yourself Chinese Myths*. London, England: Hodder & Stoughton, 2001.

born in the year of the rat are said to be talkative and clever, characteristics that the Chinese associate with rats. The cycles of the zodiac are believed to be important when making plans for the future and understanding events from the past.

Traditional Chinese cosmology seeks to explain the order of the universe. It is also populated with many minor deities, or gods, who address humans' daily concerns. These deities are believed to have been real people who developed supernatural powers, such as being able to heal disease, create rain, and battle demons, which they use on behalf of regular people with everyday problems. The Chinese gods are highly specialized; each has a certain task, role, or area of influence. They include the kitchen god, the city god, the gate god, and so on. There are gods of wealth, long life, and fire. Some twentieth-century Chinese have added Mao Zedong to this list.

Perhaps the most popular Chinese gods are the ancient Eight Immortals, dating from the Song dynasty (960–1279). They are Quan Zhongli, Zhang Guolao, Lu Dongbin, Cao Guojiu, Li Tiegua, Han Xiangzi, Lan Caihe, and He Xiangu. Each is traditionally represented holding an object that reflects his or her specialty. Cao Guojiu, patron of drama, holds castanets. Han Xiangzi, the patron of music, holds a flute. Lan Caihe, the patron of florists, carries a basket of flowers.

People pay their respects to and request favors from these deities by lighting a stick of incense before a statue or picture of the deity displayed in a public or private shrine. Then they offer a brief prayer and bow before the deity's image. If the prayer remains unanswered, the person may seek the help of another deity. If the prayer is answered, the person must repay the deity, often by burning paper money or offering him or her food, drink, or cigarettes.

A calendar wheel illustrates the Chinese zodiac. The zodiac is based on a twelve-year cycle, with each year being represented by an animal.

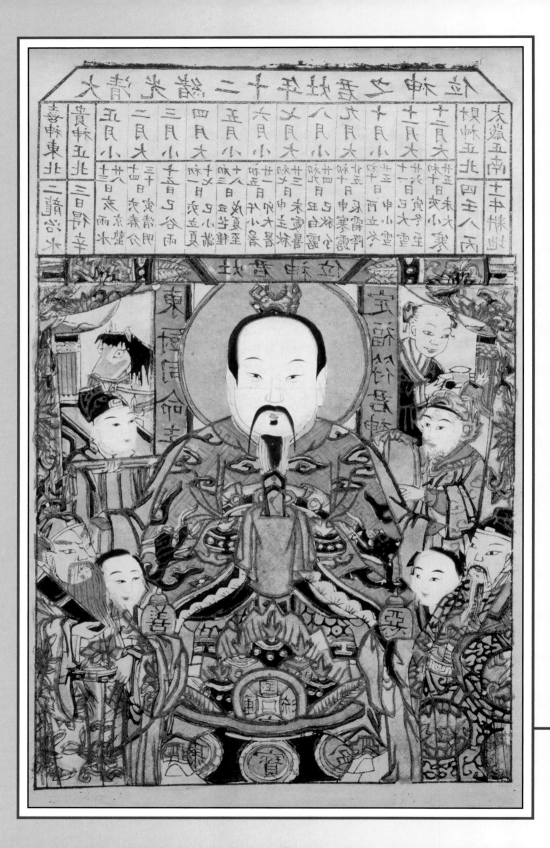

CHINESE FESTIVALS AND CEREMONIES OF ANTIQUITY AND TODAY

5

T he traditional Chinese festival calendar, based on the lunar year, was 354 or 355 days long and was divided into 12 months of 29 or 30 days. The year began on the first day of the second new moon after the winter solstice, when Earth is the greatest distance from the Sun. This day generally falls between January 21 and February 20, according to the Western calendar, known as the Gregorian calendar (named for its sixteenth-century creator, Pope Gregory XIII). The months of the year were referred to by number, not by name.

The official lunar calendar, which was calculated by court scholars, gave structure to the many festivals and celebrations of traditional Chinese life. Several festivals were held each month, usually in celebration of a folk legend or the birth of a Buddhist or Taoist deity. Several of the most ancient festivals are still celebrated today, though only one—the Spring Festival—is officially recognized by the government. It is through these ancient rituals that individuals assert their membership in a family, a community, a faith, and a people.

At left, a lunar calendar from 1895 depicts the kitchen god who, on the last day of the year, reports to the Jade Emperor—the ruler of Heaven—on the family's activities over the past year. Above, a race is underway during the annual Dragon Boat Festival, which occurs every June. In China, dragon boat racing has been drawing competitors and spectators alike for over 2,000 years. Today, it is an increasingly popular sport worldwide. Many countries, including Canada and the United States, host their own Dragon Boat Festivals.

A parade kicks off National Day celebrations on October 10 in Taipei, Taiwan. National Day commemorates the end of the Manchu dynasty and the imperial era and the formation of the Republic of China.

In addition to the popular folk festivals described in this chapter, the people of China observe eleven other important holidays: New Year's Day (January 1), Spring Festival (late January to early February), International Women's Day (March 8), Arbor Day (March 12), International Labor Day (May 1), Youth Day (May 4), International Children's Day (June 1), the anniversary of the founding of the Chinese Communist Party (July 1), Army Day (August 1), Teachers' Day (September 10), and National Day (October 1).

The New Year

Traditionally, the New Year, called *Guonian* in Chinese, marked the first day of the lunar year, which fell sometime between January 21 and February 20. In preparation for the holiday, the household came together to honor the gods. They painted lips of molasses on an image of the kitchen god and then burned the image, sending the kitchen god to the spirits to report on the family's deeds of the past year. The molasses was intended to sweeten, or improve, the story. As New Year's Day approached, everyone was encouraged to begin the new year with a clean slate. Debts were settled, relationships were renewed, and houses were cleaned. On New Year's Eve, the family displayed a new image of the kitchen god, thus welcoming him back into the household following his recent trip to the spirit world. New Year's Day was spent at home, but the following two weeks were filled with public celebrations.

In the 1910s, the Nationalist government sought to replace the traditional lunar calendar with the West's Gregorian calendar. The official celebration of the start of the

Crowds gather in a Hong Kong square to watch the dragon dances celebrating the New Year. In China, dragons are highly regarded mythic creatures that represent nobility, strength, and fortune. The Chinese dragon dance dates from more than one thousand years ago, when it was performed to ward off plague and disease.

new year was shifted to January 1, and Guonian was renamed the Spring Festival. It is called Chinese New Year by many Westerners. Today, preparation for the Spring Festival begins several weeks in advance. Many families continue the tradition of burning the kitchen god's image smeared with molasses. Some first offer the god a sticky rice cake known as *nian gao*, or "year cakes," also believed to sweeten the report delivered by the kitchen god to the spirits in heaven. Many people send greeting cards to friends and family and buy *nianhua*, which are images of deities or objects that bring good luck, to display in their homes. *Chunlian* are short poems that offer good wishes for the coming year. Many people buy small, decorative prints of these poems and paste them on doors or gates.

The celebration of the Spring Festival begins at noon on New Year's Eve. Businesses close, and people rush home. The evening is celebrated by eating rich feasts, watching public firework displays, setting off countless strings of firecrackers, and enjoying the company of family and friends. The following morning, children are given red envelopes of money called *yasuiqian*. Families spend the day offering sacrifices to ancestors, visiting temples and shrines, and watching performers act out a lion dance to scare off evil spirits, tell stories, and sing songs.

The Feast of Lanterns

Traditionally, the celebration of the new year lasts for two weeks, ending with *Deng jie*, the Feast of Lanterns, on the fifteenth day of the first month of the year. The historical origins and significance of the lantern festival are uncertain, but the observance has remained the same for centuries. Thousands of paper lanterns, some bearing clever riddles, are hung from streetlights, from the awnings of shops, and in the windows of homes. As the Sun sets, families tour the neighborhood to admire the lanterns and to be entertained by street performers. They enjoy *tanguan* or *yuanxiao*, rice flour dumplings filled with a sweet paste.

The Festival of Pure Brightness

Qingming jie, the Festival of Pure Brightness, is a time to worship and appease (satisfy) the spirits of the ancestors, a central theme in Chinese folk culture. The celebration falls on the fourth or fifth day of April. Traditionally, the entire family rises early, and, with brooms and rakes in hand, goes to the cemetery where their ancestors are buried to clean the markers and tend the grass of the family graves. Sacrifices of food and drink are made, candles and sticks of incense are lit, and ceremonial paper money is burned, representing the family's offer of valuable gifts to the ancestors. When the graves have been swept and the sacrifices have been made, the family generally enjoys a picnic nearby. Kite-flying is also traditionally associated with the Festival of Pure Brightness.

Qingming jie has lost some of its relevance in modern-day China. Cremation, once unacceptable in the culture, is now mandatory in many urban areas, where there is so little available space for burial of the dead. Instead, the ashes of the dead are

Family members gather to pay respects to their ancestors on the Festival of Pure Brightness in Hangzhou, China. Because it is a spring holiday, people like to go to the outskirts of cities to walk on the grass, fly kites, and enjoy the warm weather. For this reason, the holiday is sometimes also called Walking Amid Greenery Day.

Before the annual Full Moon Festival, Tibetan Bon pilgrims burn juniper incense as an offering to the gods. Before the arrival of Buddhism, Bon was practiced in Tibet, a once independent nation invaded by China in 1949 and under occupation ever since.

stored in public mausoleums, making the graveside rituals associated with the festival no longer necessary. However, burial is still popular among rural residents and city residents who can buy space in public cemeteries. Across the countryside, Qingming jie remains a yearly tradition with minor variations. In areas where burning fake paper money has been outlawed as a fire hazard, for example, families lay flowers by the grave marker.

The Full Moon Festival

The Mid-Autumn Festival, sometimes known as *Zhongqiu jie* (Full Moon Festival) or *Tuanyuan jie* (Reunion Festival), takes place on the fifteenth day of the eighth month of the lunar calendar (around late September in the Western calendar). The festival is a celebration of the full moon and fall harvest, a time for families to have a reunion. The Chinese word for reunion is *tuanyuan*, which literally translates as "a perfect circle." Traditionally, people celebrated the festival by making offerings, such as fruit and sweet pastries called moon cakes, to the full moon. The same rituals are performed today.

The Wedding Ceremony

Traditionally, the family has been at the core of Chinese society. Within the nuclear family (composed of parents and their children), the eldest male, usually the father, ruled the house and owned all the family property. Children helped their parents work the land or run the family business. When parents retired or the eldest son married, the father's property was divided among his male heirs, and the parents lived as dependents in their son's house. In this way, sons were dependent on their parents for protection and wealth, and parents became dependent on their sons for care and shelter in their old age. Daughters, on the other hand, received none of their parents' property, and, after marriage, were entirely dependent on their husbands and in-laws.

Tradition demanded that almost everyone marry. Men had to marry to produce male heirs who would inherit property. Women had to marry for financial security. Usually only extreme poverty would prevent a man from finding a wife, and only in very rare circumstances would a grown daughter stay in her parents' house. Given these practical concerns for young men and women, love seldom played a role in a couple's decision to marry. Professional matchmakers or female elders often arranged marriages between families, generally without the input of the young husband- and bride-to-be. Frequently, the bride and groom met for the first time at their wedding ceremony.

On the day of the wedding, the bride was dressed in red, the color of happiness. She was then carried on a sedan chair (a covered chair carried on poles) through the streets of her village, making her way from her father's house to the home of the groom's parents, where the ceremony and celebration took place. She was followed by a parade of family and friends, musicians, and men carrying her dowry. A dowry is the money, goods, or property that, in some cultures, a bride brings to her husband after getting married. A Chinese bride's traditional dowry often included pieces of furniture, articles of clothing, and other household goods.

Although the Chinese marriage ceremony differed from place to place, certain elements were standard. Neither a representative of the government nor the church presided. Instead, the couple performed simple rituals centering on food and drink. They were then pronounced married by the groom's parents, according to the regional custom. The bride kept her parents' surname but went to live in her in-laws' home. There, she would often be treated poorly until the day when she herself became a mother-in-law and had someone to look down on.

A bride, groom, and family members form a procession in a traditional Shui wedding ceremony. The Shui are an ethnic minority who live in the plains and forests of southern Guizhou Province.

If a woman found herself married to a man she did not love, as would sometimes happen in arranged marriages, she had very few options. She could not sue for divorce simply because she was unhappy or not in love. If she did manage to obtain a divorce, her chances of remarrying were slim. In addition, to avoid angering the family of the woman's husband, her father's household might refuse to welcome the divorced daughter back home. For some unhappy women, the only escape from a loveless marriage was suicide. Even in modern China, divorce is rare and frowned upon. Most unhappily married couples, however, simply learn to tolerate each other and develop separate lives.

With the Marriage Law of 1950, it became illegal to force anyone to marry. At the same time, women gained the right to seek divorce. However, arranged marriages still take place in rural areas, the last outposts of traditional culture. Most modern marriages are voluntary, though many may be based just as much on practical concerns—such as financial security—as on love. Today, couples apply for and are granted an official certificate of marriage by their local governments and are thereafter considered legally bound. As in the United States, however, this simple legal procedure has not replaced the traditional ceremony and celebration. Lavish wedding ceremonies and banquets are the order of the day, as they have been for centuries. They combine many traditions of the past—such as the bride's trip from her parents' home to that of the groom's parents—with many of the innovations of Western culture, such as an elaborate photo shoot in which the couple poses in several different outfits.

A wedding procession in Dachang, China. In a traditional Chinese wedding, which is often arranged by a matchmaker, the groom and his family pick up the bride at her home before proceeding to the ceremony.

THE RELIGIONS OF CHINA THROUGHOUT ITS HISTORY

6

Over the course of its history, China has seen the development or arrival of countless beliefs and religions. Although Confucianism remains the foundation of much Chinese tradition and thought, the People's Republic of China recognizes and allows the practice—by people over the age of eighteen, according to a 1990 law—of five religions: Taoism, Buddhism, Catholicism, Protestantism, and Islam. Many Chinese practice various folk religions, which often involve the worship of ancestors and hundreds of gods and goddesses who are thought to have influence over everyday life.

Outside of these officially accepted faiths, however, a large number of philosophies, systems of belief, and personal faiths populate China's religious landscape. Many folk religions are observed privately without intrusion from the state. Others are actively suppressed by the government. Among these is Falungong, a philosophy that draws its inspiration from Buddhism, Taoism, the words of Falungong founder Li Hongzhi, and the practice of *qigong* (see chapter 10). In 1999, the Chinese government banned Falungong, describing it as a superstitious cult.

The Feng-Hsien Temple *(left)* is a seventh-century BC monastery carved out of the surrounding hillside in Longmen, China. Above the temple looms a massive carving of the Buddha. Above, a priest burns incense in the Man Mo Temple, which was built in 1840 and is one of Hong Kong's oldest Taoist temples. It is dedicated to the god of literature and the god of war.

This portrait of Confucius is carved on a stone slab dating from the Tang dynasty (AD 618–907). Confucius taught that charity, love, and kindness were among the highest virtues and loving and respecting one's neighbors the highest human duty.

Confucianism

The most influential thinker of China's ancient past was Kongfuzi, known to Westerners as Confucius. Confucius lived from 551 to 479 BC, a period of great political and social instability that produced an explosion of philosophical debate. Central to Confucius's thought was a deep respect for traditional values and rituals. Confucius felt these were not simply relics from the past but the foundation of a modern understanding of the world. The past, Confucius believed, could teach people basic principles. When absorbed and interpreted by the individual, these principles could serve as a guide for answering life's difficult questions and for addressing contemporary problems.

Confucius also supported a hierarchical society, in which social and political power is structured like a layered pyramid. The emperor would be on top, and below him in descending order of power members of his court, civil servants, land owners, farmers, and servants. Families were structured in a similar way, with the father as the head, followed by the mother, sons, and daughters. Each person in society was expected to meet the social

A cave near the ancient town of Qufu where Confucius was born is considered a holy site by those who follow his teachings.

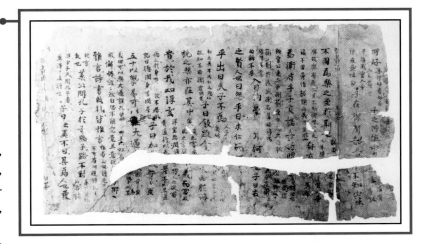

In 1967, a piece of hemp paper bearing Chinese characters from the *Analects of Confucius (right)* was found near Turfan in Xinjiang Province in a tomb dated to AD 1100.

obligations of his or her role, whether emperor, subject, landlord, farmer, master, servant, father, mother, son, daughter, wife, or husband.

These social roles are learned, not instinctive, so Confucianism places great importance on education. Confucius also felt that people did not have to remain at the social level to which they were born but could move up and down the social ladder. Therefore, self-improvement and social mobility are also important elements in Confucianism. According to Confucianism, everyone is capable of achieving perfection, of becoming a *junzi*, or "superior man," and a leader in society. The superior man was a model of good behavior, integrity, reciprocity (giving back as much as you receive), loyalty, and humanity.

Because Confucius was an agnostic (one who does not commit to the belief of either the existence or nonexistence of God), he preferred to consider the questions of the earthly world and how best to live one's life in it. For this reason, Confucianism is not a religion in the traditional sense. It has no priests or ministers and does not refer to gods, the spirit world, or the afterlife. It is a way of understanding human existence through the creation of a series of guidelines for how to live and fulfill one's social responsibilities.

Taoism

Another philosophy to emerge from the turmoil of the Zhou dynasty was Taoism. Taoism is a mystical religion based on the idea of Tao, which translates as "way" or "road." The Tao is an eternal, formless, nameless thing, and reverence for it is a reverence for personal freedom and the laws of nature. In a Taoist world view, it is not natural for humans to be confined by human laws, inhibitions (social anxieties), or

A sixteenth-century Ming dynasty ink-on-silk painting depicts Laozi riding his ox. The ox represents a spiritual vehicle, or "the way." The goal of Taoism, founded by Laozi in the sixth century BC, is to bring all elements of existence—heaven, Earth, humans—into harmony.

social customs, which only serve to stunt individuality. Human desire is good, and life should be pleasurable. In an ideal and peaceful society, according to Taoism, people would ignore convention and act only on their instincts and desires. Government would be unnecessary in such a society because people would govern themselves, and the choices they would make would not harm themselves or their neighbors. Within Taoism, however, there does exist a hierarchy of otherworldly deities (gods) and human clergy.

The guiding text of Taoism, known as the Laozi or the Taodejing, is a complex exploration of these ideas by the Old Master of Taoism, Laozi. When and by whom these writings were compiled, and whether Laozi ever existed, is unknown. Not surprisingly, given its rejection of the need for government, Taoism never acquired much official support or recognition. It did have a profound effect on Chinese culture, however, especially on art, literature, and folk religion.

Buddhism

Buddhism originated in the sixth century BC. An Indian prince, known as Siddhartha or Sakyamuni, left home at the age of twenty-nine in search of enlightenment. It came one day as he meditated under a bodhi tree. He became known as the Buddha, "the enlightened one." The Buddha began to teach the keys to enlightenment, known as the Four Noble Truths, to a growing number of followers.

An elderly Chinese Taoist priest smiles for the camera. Taoism, still widely practiced in China, has also become increasingly popular in Western countries.

The Great Buddha of Leshan is the largest Buddha statue in the world. It stands 233 feet (71 m) tall and 92 feet (28 m) wide. Its foot is 30 feet (9 m) wide and 36 feet (11 m) long so that nearly 100 people can sit on it.

Life, the Buddha preached, is made of suffering, which is caused by desire. Salvation is possible only by overcoming and letting go of one's desires. All thinking creatures are caught in the cycle of death and rebirth. We are reborn as high or low creatures depending on our karma—the accumulation of good or bad deeds over the course of our lives. In order to be reborn as higher creatures, we must give up the material pleasures of life and dedicate ourselves to restoring our karma. In doing so, we may even reach the heavenly paradise, called nirvana, and be released from the cycle of birth, death, and rebirth altogether.

Buddhism first appeared in China during the Han dynasty (202 BC–AD 220) and first became influential, both as a religious and a political force, between the fourth and the ninth centuries AD. Its message appealed to a wide cross-section of society, including peasants, landlords, and even the emperor. Buddhist temples and monasteries were soon being built across China.

Today, Buddhism remains an important part of Chinese culture. There are more than 13,000 Buddhist temples in China. In Tibet and Inner Mongolia, Buddhists practice a form of their faith known as Lamaism, which is quite separate from

Young Buddhist monks read scripture at a monastery in Lhasa, Tibet. The spiritual leader of the Tibetan Buddhists is the Dalai Lama, who is believed to be a reincarnation of the Buddha of Compassion. Following China's occupation of Tibet, the Dalai Lama fled to India where he runs the Tibetan government-in-exile.

Matteo Ricci was an Italian priest who founded a Jesuit mission along the Silk Road in China in the late sixteenth century.

Buddhism as it is known in southern and eastern China. Before the Chinese invasion of Tibet in 1959, which forced the Dalai Lama (the spiritual and political leader of Lamaism) to find refuge in India and brought Tibet under Chinese rule, Lamaism was the foundation of Tibet's theocratic, or religion-based, government.

Christianity

The rise of Christianity in China dates from the sixth and seventh centuries AD and the arrival of Christian Persian merchants along the silk routes of western China. By the mid-ninth century, however, Christianity was outlawed in China because it was foreign and therefore to be mistrusted.

Christianity would not see a revival in China until the sixteenth century, when missionaries arrived, hoping to convert the emperor himself. They were not successful. In the mid-nineteenth century, a new generation of Christian missionaries flocked to China. They enjoyed some success, but they were associated with the West and with the imperialism of the major foreign powers. Many Chinese saw the missionaries as the frontline troops of an imperialism that would result in the domination of their country by Western nations.

Today, like other state-sanctioned religions in China, Christianity is highly regulated. China's 12,000 Protestant churches report to the administrative body known as the Three-Self Patriotic Movement. The Chinese Catholic Church, numbering some four million members, is supervised by the Chinese Catholic Patriotic Association. The Roman Catholic Church, however, is outlawed in China, because it is "controlled" by a foreign power, namely the Vatican. The Roman Catholic Church continues to operate in secret, however, and claims some 10 million members.

Islam

Islam is a religion founded on the belief in one god, Allah, and his prophet Muhammad. The word of Allah, as recorded by Muhammad, is recorded in the Koran, the sacred text of Islam. Muslims, people who practice Islam, engage in organized prayer five times per day. In accordance with the Koran, observant Muslims keep a strict diet, wear traditional dress and head coverings, and, if possible, journey to the holy city of Mecca, the birthplace of Muhammad. This pilgrimage is called the *hajj*.

Like Christianity, Islam was brought to China by the Persian and Arab merchants of the seventh century AD. At first, the Muslim merchants maintained their religious and cultural traditions. Over time, however, many Muslims assimilated to the Chinese way of life, and many Chinese embraced Islam through marriage to Muslims and conversion to their faith.

Today, there are roughly 30,000 mosques (temples) in China. The largest Muslim communities in China are in the outlying autonomous regions, in particular the Xinjiang Uygar Autonomous Region and the Ningxia Hui Autonomous Region. There are also large Muslim communities in provinces historically dominated by Han Chinese, including Yunnan and Gansu.

The Chinese city of Linxia in the southeast Gansu Province is known as the Mecca of China for its great number of mosques and large Muslim population. Linxia's Muslim roots can be traced back nearly 1,000 years when it was a major stop for Arab merchants traveling along the Silk Road. Above, Muslim worshippers throng to one of Linxia's large mosques.

THE ART AND ARCHITECTURE OF CHINA

7

On a brief trip through 5,000 years of Chinese art, we will encounter three major developments in the artists' media (the tools they used to create their work). The earliest medium was clay, followed by bronze, and then by the "arts of the brush," calligraphy and painting. The appearance of each new medium did not signal the end of previous ones. Instead, older techniques and materials were adapted and expanded to meet the artistic possibilities presented by the new technology.

Chinese architecture, at least until the twentieth century, was less marked by dramatic change and innovation than were the fine arts of painting, printmaking, and sculpting. From the fifteenth century through the end of the imperial age, the techniques and materials that architects used to build monumental structures did not change much. Large-scale Chinese architecture did not undergo the dramatic developmental periods that characterize European and American construction of the same time period. The only major variations in Chinese design were the ornamental accents (such as sculptures and carvings). This is not to say that there was no variety in Chinese architecture. Differences in building styles, though, tended to be based on regional variations, climate considerations, available building materials and wealth, and the lifestyles of the occupants rather than the time period.

At left: In 1974, while digging a well near X'ian, China, farmers discovered more than 8,000 life-sized terra-cotta (baked clay) soldiers, 96 horses, and 11 chariots buried in the ground. This clay army "guarded" the imperial tomb of China's first emperor, Qin Shihuangdi (259–210 BC). Each of the 8,000 figures is individually sculpted, with its own style of dress, weaponry, and facial expression. They even stand in proper military formation. Above, the Forbidden City in Beijing is a city-palace that stretches more than 861,113 square yards (720,000 square m) and has 800 buildings that together contain 9,000 rooms.

The Great Wall of China stretches almost 4,000 miles (6,400 km) from the Korean border on the Yalu River to the Gobi Desert. Parts of the wall are in severe need of repair. Only recently, after much campaigning by the Chinese Great Wall Society, has the Chinese government passed laws designed to protect the historic landmark.

On the dry, cold northern plains, for example, there are people who live deep under ground to this day, seeking shelter from the cold and wind. In the wet, hot southern reaches of the country, on the other hand, people live in houses on stilts to escape floodwaters and catch cooling breezes.

Chinese artists and architects have created monumental works of art that celebrate the nation and its government as well as beautiful objects and structures that have practical everyday uses. In this way, the history of art in China offers insight into the lives of the nation and its people throughout their long, shared history.

Clay

The earliest examples modern archaeologists and art historians have of China's long artistic history are Neolithic period (6000–1500 BC) clay pots dating from roughly 3000 BC. Excavations of the ruins of early villages along the banks of the Yellow River have unearthed well-preserved artifacts from this period. The people of these villages

This Chinese vase from the Neolithic era (6000–1500 BC) was created by the Yangshao. The Yangshao lived in the mountainous regions of northern and western China and created pottery with geometric designs painted on them.

lived in small circular huts that were divided into cramped living areas by posts in the ground. The walls and roof were made of wooden ribs covered with a thick layer of thatch. The village also had a community house, a burial ground some distance away, and potters' workshops complete with kilns, or ovens, used to bake the soft clay into hard, watertight vessels.

Most commonly, these villagers made coil pots by molding rough gray clay into a long, snakelike cord and coiling the clay in the shape of a bowl or jug. Some potters, however, transformed these common clay vessels into an art form. They developed finer, more delicate, and more decorative pieces of burnished or painted pottery. These pieces were often covered in symbols and realistic or abstract images of creatures. The most experimental potters were members of a group known only as the Black Pottery people, named for the color of the baked pottery they made. Not only did the Black Potters polish their pieces until the clay shone, they also developed unusual shapes for their vessels. They experimented with glazes and firing techniques to make their pieces, often pear-shaped vases and shallow dishes, as elegant and delicate as possible.

Bronze

Bronze crafts and tools were first developed in China around the eighteenth century BC. Bronze is an alloy, or mixture, of copper and tin, to which the Chinese added lead, a unique variation seen only in Chinese bronze work.

This ritual elephant-shaped vase dating from the second millennium BC was probably used for burning incense or dried flowers.

At the site of the earliest Shang city, dating from the sixteenth century BC, archaeologists found large workshops for bronze casting, stone carving, and pottery. The artifacts found there, all objects made for the priest-king rulers, show that the Shang people were experimenting with the new technology of bronze casting in varied and unusual ways. Examples include a bowl in the shape of a stout, wrinkled rhinoceros; a tall, slender goblet with a mouth like a trumpet; and a lidded bucket in the shape of a monster grasping a terrified human. Much of the bronze work from the Shang period, especially ceremonial objects, is covered with textures, patterns, and symbols.

The Arts of the Brush and Ink

The Qin (221–202 BC) and Han (202 BC–AD 220) dynasties saw the rise of a new form of artistic expression in China. The artists of this period developed and perfected what are known as the arts of the brush and ink—calligraphy and painting. The brush was made of animal fur or the barbs of a feather attached to the end of a bamboo stick. The ink was made of pine carbon, glue, and water. The calligrapher knew how to move the brush in careful, steady strokes, how to arrange the written characters across the painting's imagery, and how the paper would absorb the ink. The earliest paintings of this period were done on the walls of tombs and on cloth banners used in burial rituals. They depicted mythical representations of the heavens and everyday scenes of earthly life.

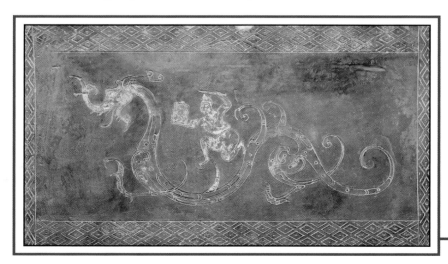

A Han dynasty (202 BC–AD 220) tomb plaque depicts a warrior riding a dragon. Unlike Western dragon myths, in China dragons are thought to be kind, generous creatures who control the rain and allow the crops to grow.

A tenth-century painting on silk illustrates the "Ten Levels of the Bodhisattva," a section from the Avatamsaka sutra. The Avatamsaka or Flower Wreath sutra is one of the most influential texts in Eastern Buddhist traditions and discusses the deeds of the Buddha and their merits that blossom like a garland of flowers.

The Influence of Buddhist Missionaries

The first Buddhist missionaries arrived in China during the Qin and Han dynasties, and their influence on Chinese architecture and decorative arts was powerful. Bronze, which had become overshadowed by the developments made in ceramics, enjoyed a brief return to popularity as early as the fourth century AD, when figurines used in public and private Buddhist shrines were cast in bronze. The Chinese also adopted the Buddhist practice of recording texts and images on paper and silk hand scrolls. Painters adopted the bright, colorful palette of Indian art and painted bold scenes of the Buddha on long, hanging scrolls. Buddhist symbols were incorporated into secular (nonreligious) paintings. Chinese temples, both Confucian and Taoist, were built in the style of Indian Buddhist temples.

Chinese Buddhist temples from this period were walled compounds that contained several separate buildings. The structures were built of wood pillars and crossbeams. Roofs were tiled. The design and the materials used to build these

The Zhang Fei Temple in Yuyang was built in honor of Zhang Fei, a third-century general murdered by lower-ranking soldiers. When the Three Gorges Dam now being built on the Yangtze River is finished, the flood waters will completely cover the temple.

temples were traditional Chinese, based on the earliest palaces. However, the influence of Buddhist missionaries can be seen in the introduction of the pagoda, a kind of temple. In India, these structures were single-story buildings constructed around a central pillar. In China, pagodas rose ten or twelve stories with an upward curved roof atop each story. Long ago, the earliest examples of these Buddhist pagodas rotted in neglect or were destroyed by the imperial state, which was determined to stamp out Buddhism. However, temples built in Japan in the following centuries were faithful to the original Chinese plans and give modern observers a suggestion of what the earliest Chinese Buddhist pagodas looked like.

Art and Architecture of the Imperial Age

Calligraphy and painting would become China's most celebrated art forms during the imperial era. Painters had been exposed to the great possibilities of the medium, and they responded with a flurry of vivid, experimental work that continues to this day. They broadened the range of colors in their palettes. They played with perspective, so viewers saw the details of the artists' landscape paintings in new and fresh ways.

Most famously, imperial-era artists blended calligraphy and painting, creating works that combined written characters and images. In the fourth century, an artist named Gu Kaizhi emerged as a master of narrative (story-telling) painting. In his work, each section of a longhand scroll told a different part of a legendary story. In the tenth century,

Fan Kuan was a Taoist painter during the Song dynasty (AD 960–1279). At left is his painting entitled *Snowy Landscape*. This painting, like most of his work, reflects the Taoist belief that human beings should be one with nature.

Horse and Groom in Winter by Chao Meng-Fu (1254–1322) displays the artist's most famous gift—his delicate depictions of animals and humans. Chao is also famous for his calligraphy, which is considered some of the best from the Yüan dynasty (1271–1368).

the artists Zhu Ran and Fan Kuan popularized paintings of rocky mountain passes on long, hanging scrolls. The themes of space and monumental natural wonders took on great importance in Chinese landscape painting. In the twelfth century, Emperor Hui Zong introduced and led a new school of painting that focused on small scenes of nature depicted in painstaking detail. The most famous painter from this period was Zhao Mengfu. The fourteenth through seventeenth centuries saw the experimental blending of all of these styles in the elegant, often quirky, landscapes of Qian Xuan, Ni Zan, Wu Zhen, and Shen Zhou.

Around this time, emperors began building the palaces, tombs, and temples that mark the height of traditional Chinese architecture. The most famous of these is the imperial palace in Beijing, known as the Forbidden City. This massive structure was begun by the third emperor of the Ming dynasty, Yongle, in 1406. It would be added to and reconstructed by his successors. Today, it is known as the Palace Museum.

The Forbidden City's palace compound includes a series of buildings, all facing south, one

The Forbidden City in Beijing is blanketed by a snowfall. The Forbidden City, a royal palace from 1406 until 1912, is home to many artifacts and treasures. In 1947, many of the artifacts were moved by the Nationalists and now form a large part of the collection of the National Palace Museum in Taipei, Taiwan.

Porcelain was first made in China, which is why porcelain goods are sometimes called "china." Ming vases, like the one at left, were glazed blue and white. Sometimes they were then painted over with enamel colors and decorative figures, such as dragons and phoenixes, animals, plants, and humans.

behind the other and separated by huge courtyards and tall gates. A thick wall, which itself houses meeting rooms, offices, living quarters, and gardens, surrounds the compound and opens at several gates. The southernmost gate opens onto Tian'anmen Square, or Heavenly Gate Square. In all, the Forbidden City includes roughly 10,000 structures, a canal, and three lakes. The buildings are all built of wooden pillars and beams supported by a stone foundation with roofs made of yellow glazed tile.

Modern and Contemporary Chinese Art and Architecture

The rise of modern China, marked by the arrival of the first European traders, diplomats, and missionaries in the seventeenth and eighteenth centuries, set off the large-scale production of Chinese wares, known as *chinoiserie*, for foreign markets. The influence of foreign styles can be seen in ceramic work and paintings of this period, as Chinese artisans strove both to exploit their traditional design and incorporate the tastes and styles of the European consumer. Perhaps the most famous of China's highly decorated ceramicware are the porcelain vases and bowls of the Ming dynasty. These pieces were produced in imperial factories. They are often white and blue and show scenes of birds and flowers. More elaborate landscapes in a full rainbow of colors were also produced in the imperial kilns. The making and selling of chinoserie continued throughout the nineteenth and early twentieth centuries.

As early as 1911, the Nationalist government initiated a policy that forced artists to produce propaganda for the state. The Chinese Communist Party continued this policy. All state-sponsored artists were required to complete official art training.

Many of them were sent to study in the Soviet Union, while Soviet artists came to China to teach the dominant Soviet style of artistic propaganda, a style called socialist realism. Artists, particularly painters and printmakers, were strongly encouraged to produce art that "served the people" by teaching them about Chinese history and Communist doctrine, celebrating the revolution and workers' struggles, and pointing toward a socialist paradise in the near future. Punishment for the creation of work that was judged to be out of step with the goals of revolution and the Communist Party was often harsh, even deadly. Artists were often sent to the country for hard labor or were imprisoned, exiled, or executed for their work.

A nineteenth-century painting depicts three Chinese men making silk. It is believed that the art of silkmaking in China can be traced at least as far back as 5,500 years ago. Raw silk comes from silkworm cocoons, and Chinese cultivation of the silkworm can be traced from the third century BC. The famous Silk Road to the Middle East and Europe started with the efforts of Chinese explorer Zhang Qian to trade silk to Persia in the second century BC.

The Communist Party believed that traditional artists were out of touch with the modern world and the daily life of workers. In order to satisfy the government, Chinese painters began using Western oil paints and creating monumental, heroic portraits of party leaders, scenes of peasants at work, and depictions of political events from recent history. Landscapes, birds, and flowers were

Above, the Communist Party Congress meets in the Great Hall of the People in Beijing on November 14, 2002. The Great Hall of the People was built by Communist volunteers in only ten months between 1958 and 1959. Larger in area than the Forbidden City, the hall can seat all 10,000 representatives of China's parliament while also hosting 5,000 guests in a banquet hall. It contains 300 meeting halls, lounges, and office rooms.

strictly off-limits, unless the work was based on one of Mao Zedong's poems or had some similar link to the party and its program. Printmaking, especially humble woodblock printing, became popular as the art form of the people because it was earthy, straightforward, and often black-and-white.

Architects were also forced to promote the party's political agenda in their work. They were given somewhat more creative freedom, however, particularly during the Great Leap Forward. One of the most celebrated examples of Chinese Communist-era architecture is Beijing's Great Hall of the People, where China's legislature, the National People's Congress, meets. The Great Hall was built in ten months by Communist volunteers during 1958 and 1959. It stands on the west side of Tian'anmen Square. Containing more floor area (1,829,865 square feet [170,000 square m]) than the Forbidden City, the hall can simultaneously seat all 10,000 representatives of China's parliament while entertaining 5,000 guests in a banquet hall. For this reason, the hall is sometimes referred to as "the ten thousand people's meeting hall." It has 300 meeting halls, lounges, and office rooms.

Hong Kong is divided into four main areas—Kowloon, Hong Kong Island *(right)*, the New Territories, and the Outlying Islands. Kowloon and the New Territories are on a peninsula of the Chinese mainland. Hong Kong Island is on the southern side of the harbor facing Kowloon. The city itself is centered around the harbor.

Each meeting hall is named for one of China's provinces, municipalities, or autonomous regions and decorated in the local style appropriate to that region. On the roof of the Great Hall sits a huge red star, the main symbol of Communist China.

With the reforms of the late 1970s, artists once again came to enjoy greater freedom of expression. Many Chinese artists have rediscovered the traditional arts of brush and ink, which they have applied to traditional and abstract subject matter. Working with oil paint, others have explored the problems of the past and present by incorporating realistic figures in fictional situations. Once uncommon genres—lithography (a type of printing), mixed media (the combination of two or more media, such as painting and video), and installation pieces (work designed to be shown in a gallery or other specific space)—have also taken root in China's modern art scene.

Architecturally, China is growing in new and exciting ways. Increasingly crowded cities demand innovations in large-scale construction. Most often the problems of overcrowding and underfunding are solved by building huge, unattractive, steel and concrete structures ranging in size from four-story apartment houses to high-rise housing projects and monolithic government agencies. However, there are many exceptions to this rule, as Chinese architects are finding creative solutions to tight space and even tighter funds. In the stylistically varied suburban homes outside the coastal cities, the traditional mud-brick homes of the villages, the gray tile buildings in the centers of small towns, and the new, brick developments of growing cities, Chinese architects are heading into the twenty-first century by drawing inspiration from the past while attempting to perceive the shape and needs of the future.

THE LITERATURE AND MUSIC OF CHINA

8

Throughout its ancient and imperial history, China fostered the development of two main genres of literature: popular literature and classical Confucian texts. Since the earliest days of Chinese civilization, popular literature has thrived. Before the advent of woodblock printing and paper, a rich tradition of folklore was passed from one generation to the next and from village to village through informal storytelling. The earliest known record of Chinese writing, dating from the Shang dynasty (1766–1122 BC), took the form of questions posed to the spirits carved on bones and shells. The bones and shells were then scorched with fire. The resulting cracks that formed on their surfaces were interpreted by diviners (fortunetellers). This practice was called scapulimancy. Although the simple scrawled questions are not considered early examples of Chinese literature, these artifacts do give anthropologists an interesting peek at the concerns of everyday life and early Chinese writing.

Early Chinese Fiction

The first known Chinese short stories, which drew their inspiration and often their plots from

At left, an opera singer performs traditional Chinese opera on a Beijing stage in 1995. Chinese opera performers wear elaborate folk costumes and heavily paint their faces to resemble masks. The Beijing Opera performs works based on historical novels about military battles and political struggles. Above, a young Chinese child plays the *p'i-p'a*, a stringed instrument similar to a guitar or lute. In China, music is considered one of the most important parts of an early education. Chinese children often begin music lessons as early as three and four years old.

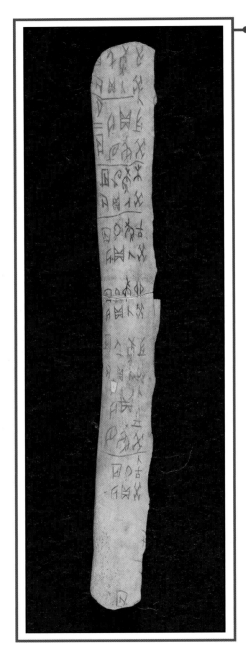

A Chinese oracle bone from the Shang dynasty (1766–1122 BC). Oracle bones were turtle shells inscribed with Chinese characters that listed questions on harvests, wars, and other questions of public concern. The bones were then heated up until cracks began to appear. The cracks were then interpreted as answers to the inscribed questions. Sometimes the supposed answers were then also carved into the bones.

the stories of ancient oral folklore, were composed during the Tang dynasty (AD 618–907). The first novels appeared during the Yüan dynasty (AD 1271–1368), when unemployed intellectuals, unable to find work after the abolition of civil service examinations, decided to apply their classical education to writing literature in the vernacular, or common, informal language. Yüan-era texts could be reproduced in greater numbers thanks to new printing technology. They were read with great interest and enthusiasm by the increasingly literate populations of the growing coastal cities.

The novel was the direct descendant of the ancient tradition of storytelling. Novels such as *Shuihu Zhuan* (*The Water Margin*, c. fourteenth century), and Lo Guanzhong's *Sanguozhi Yanyi* (*The Romance of the Three Kingdoms*, c. fifteenth century), draw on the ancient romance cycles that storytellers had retold countless times over many hundreds of years. Though the names of most imperial-era novelists are lost to history, their texts survive. These novels offer a glimpse into contemporary Chinese life because the stories feature relatively realistic characters.

Novels, and the people who wrote them, were often condemned by dynastic bureaucrats, who felt threatened by the novels' mass popularity and use of everyday language. Because they owed their success and power to years of education, the obtaining of special knowledge, and the use of the formal court language, these bureaucrats felt

undermined by popular literature. To preserve their own positions in society, imperial officials instead celebrated the texts of that great upholder of tradition, Confucius.

The Confucian Canon

The classical Confucian texts date from the Zhou dynasty (c. sixteenth century BC). One of the great cultural developments of the Han era was the canonization of *Wujing*, or the *Five Classics*. Canonization refers to the process a ruling body or influential group of people uses to create an officially approved list of books and other texts. The *Five Classics* include *Shujing (Classic of History), Chunqiu (Spring and Autumn Annals), Yijing (Classic of Changes), Shijing (Classic of Poetry),* and *Liji (Classic of Rites).*

During the Song dynasty (960–1279), neo-Confucian philosopher Zhu Xi added four more texts, known as *Sishu,* or the *Four Books,* to the canon: *Daxue,* from the *Classic of Rites; Zhongyong,* from the *Doctrine of the Mean; Lunyü,* or the *Analects;*

Above is an illustrated page from Luo Guanzhong's fourteenth-century epic novel *The Romance of the Three Kingdoms*. The novel details the end of the Han dynasty at the hands of the three rebellious kingdoms of Wei, Shu, and Wu, and the three heroes who fight unsuccessfully to protect and save the country. *The Romance of the Three Kingdoms* continues to be one of China's most popular novels and is still widely read.

The *Five Classics* were written during the Zhou dynasty by rulers and government officials. Though they are sometimes referred to as the Confucian Classics, they were not written by Confucius. The five books represent the entire educational program for the young men of the ruling and educated classes. Each book covers one of the important artistic or spiritual disciplines, including divination, history, poetry, philosophy, and ritual.

and *Mengzi*, or the *Book of Mencius*. Other texts, including *Xiaojing*, or the *Classic of Filial Piety*, were considered central to a well-rounded imperial education. *Xiaojing* is said to be the record of a conversation between Confucius and one of his followers. The oldest surviving versions of these texts are copies that date from the invention of the woodblock printing process during the Song dynasty. Earlier versions, made by scratching characters on loosely bound strips of wood or bamboo, are lost. These early books were cumbersome and fragile.

Shijing, the *Classic of Poetry* or the *Book of Songs*, is the oldest known example of recorded literature. It was compiled sometime between 1000 BC and 600 BC. The *Shijing* is a collection of some 300 anonymous poems. It is considered an early example of popular literature because many of the poems deal with the loves and lives of everyday folk. Despite its popular tone and themes, though, Confucian-era scholars adored it, not for its subject matter but simply because the poems were so old. As discussed earlier, Confucianism places great value on the traditions and lessons of the past.

Twentieth-Century Chinese Literature

For many centuries, Confucian texts written in classic wén-yán Chinese dominated Chinese literature, especially in the schools. However, scholars of the 1910s and the 1920s, notably Hu Shi and Lu Xun, began to campaign for the revival of vernacular literature. Readers who did not have the specialized, formal education found the classic texts increasingly difficult to understand.

Many, including Lu, believed that the small amount of new literature that was being produced failed to reflect or address the problems of the age. The people of China were facing crises at home and abroad. The revolution had succeeded. Two thousand years of dynastic rule had come to a sudden end, leaving the new Nationalist government to create a republic from its ruins. In Europe, World War I raged and threatened to engulf China and possibly lead to the carving up of its lands among the warring Western nations. Lu and many of his colleagues continued to praise traditional culture, but they also called for pioneering new styles of modern literature that would be accessible to the common man and woman and reflect their turbulent lives. In 1918, Lu wrote the first vernacular short story, entitled "Kuangren riji" ("Diary of a Madman"), which was published in the revolutionary journal *Xin Qingnian* (*New Youth*).

Above is an illustration from "The Ode of Chen," one of the poems in the *Shijing (Book of Odes)*, China's earliest collection of poetry. The *Shijing* is a collection of 305 songs, poems, and hymns dating from the Zhou dynasty to the Spring and Autumn period (770–476 BC). The collection, supposedly collected and edited by Confucius, is divided into four main sections: poems or songs about ordinary people, the nobility, and rulers; and ceremonial religious hymns.

Lu Xun is often called the father of modern Chinese literature. He wrote the first Chinese short story ever written in bái-huà, the language of ordinary people, entitled "Diary of a Madman."

At his death in 1936, Lu Xun's career was celebrated by the Chinese Communist Party, which praised his revolutionary spirit and what they saw as his complete rejection of traditional, elite art forms. The party's attitude toward literature was that it should serve as a tool for teaching party ideology. As early as 1942, in his "Talks at the Yannan Forum on Art and Literature," Mao Zedong criticized elitist intellectuals and urged them to study the "common man" in order to create a truly revolutionary literature, one that conveyed the "proletarian standpoint" (the perspective of the working classes).

Yet even though the Communist Party was promoting a revolution in literature, it was not at all interested in intellectual freedom. Writers who criticized the Communist Party or revolutionary society were punished. Many were sent to work in factories or on farms. Others were imprisoned, and still others were executed. The most widely circulated book during the period of the Cultural Revolution was the so-called Little Red Book, a pocket-sized collection of brief sayings and slogans taken from Mao Zedong's writings. Some 100 millions copies of the book, entitled *Quotations from Chairman Mao*, were printed and sold, and it became a kind of sacred and required text for most Chinese.

At left is the jacket of Lu Xun's second collection of short stories, *Wandering*, published in 1926. The cover was designed by Tao Yuanqing, a famous Chinese artist.

Chinese Literature Today

Deng Xiaoping's reforms of the late 1970s brought an end to the censorship of literature by the state. Initially, writers proceeded with some caution, careful to test the limits of this new freedom. As time passed, however, Chinese writers became increasingly experimental and controversial.

Several schools of writing have developed in the last twenty-five years. The first, known as scar literature, chronicled the injustices of the Cultural Revolution. In the 1980s, a second new genre of literature developed around a reverence for ancient philosophies and rituals, which were seen as the essence of Chinese culture. Authors such as Mo Yan turned their attention to the countryside, the birthplace of Chinese tradition. The countryside, and by extension Chinese culture, was depicted as both beautiful and ugly, mystical and everyday. Accompanying this renewed interest in ancient Chinese culture was a popular obsession with all things Western. Translations of American and European texts became available and popular. The classics of

Soldiers of the Chinese People's Liberation Army recite from Mao Zedong's Little Red Book in April 1970. During the Great Cultural Revolution, every Chinese citizen was required to own this collection of Mao's sayings. If a person failed to produce a copy of the book upon request, he or she could be punished severely and sent to a labor camp.

Gao Xingjian won the Nobel Prize for Literature in 2000. He is not only a writer but also a painter, director, dramatist, and translator. Because he writes of the often harsh realities of life in Communist China, his work is banned there. In 1987, he left China and eventually settled in Paris.

Western theater, twentieth-century fiction, psychology texts, romance novels, and political histories were all translated and sold to an eager Chinese readership.

A third genre of modern Chinese literature is more experimental than either scar or rural literature, often ignoring the rules of grammar, form, and logic. Perhaps the most celebrated member of this movement is Gao Xingjiang, who, in 2000, became the first Chinese to win the Nobel Prize for literature.

In the last decade, Chinese literature has undergone yet another dramatic shift, away from the experimental and toward the commercial. The publishing industry has blossomed, and countless popular authors have built successful careers by meeting the demands of a mass audience. Popular novels, especially martial arts stories, enjoy great success.

Classical Music

Traditional Chinese music is very different from its Western counterparts. The sound is thin and high-pitched, compared to the full and deep sound of classical Western music. In addition, the various musicians in a traditional Chinese ensemble adjust their instruments to different pitches, resulting in an overall sound that would strike a Western listener as being out of tune. Rhythm and harmony are relatively unimportant in traditional Chinese music. The melody of the piece is paramount.

Traditional Chinese music is played on a wide variety of instruments. From the resonant gong to the high-pitched *suona* (a reed instrument), these instruments produce a range of sounds that can evoke a wide range of emotions. Many of the instruments that have survived into the twenty-first century—as artifacts, images in

These traditional Chinese musical instruments are *(from left to right)*: the *Hu-chin* and bow, the *sheng* (a pipe-like instrument), the three-stringed *san-hsien*, and the p'i-p'a, or balloon guitar.

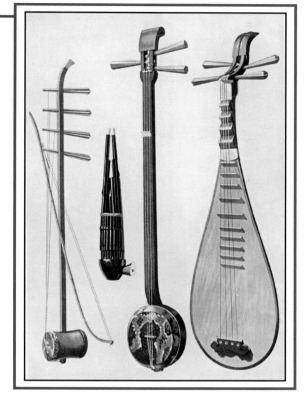

paintings, or references in classical texts—are not native to China, but the Chinese have incorporated them into a rich musical tradition that is distinctly Chinese.

Among the traditional instruments that remain popular today is the four-stringed, teardrop-shaped lute, called the *p'i-p'a*. It first appeared in China during the Han dynasty but probably originated in the Middle East sometime before that. Another popular stringed instrument is the *erhu*, which has its origins in central Asia and became popular in China around the fourteenth century. Two strings are attached at the head and foot of a long, slender neck. The bow rests between the two strings. As with the violin, the musician draws the bow across the strings to produce sound. A third instrument that has enjoyed popularity in China since the imperial age is the *suona*, which originated in India or central Asia and first appeared in China in the sixteenth century. The suona is a reed instrument with a thin wooden body that ends in a large brass or copper horn.

These instruments and the sounds they produce have been an important part of daily life in China for centuries. For example, the suona was blown to muster imperial troops and to set the beat of the daily march to the fields on 1950s agricultural collectives. Today, the suona can still be heard in wedding and funeral marches and at the opera, where it signals the entrance on stage of the actor playing the emperor.

Chinese Opera

Chinese opera is a combination of song, dance, spoken dialogue, gymnastics, and martial arts blended together to tell Confucian stories of good and evil. A descendant of

A 1,000-year-old opera is performed in the city of Qiatou, in China's western mountains of Yunnan Province. The actors wear traditional costumes and dramatic face paint and sing a traditional folk song, "Giu Er Xi." The audience is encouraged to sing along.

ancient pantomimes set to music, Chinese opera first gained widespread popularity during the thirteenth century AD. For many centuries thereafter, it dominated popular entertainment.

A trip to the opera during the imperial era was a lively all-day event. Operas were staged in open spaces, in temples, at street markets, and in elegant theaters. Food and drink were served, gossip was shared, and great battles, tragic legends, and comic tales were acted and sung on stage. The dawn of the twentieth century saw a decline in traditional opera because of the revolutionary cultural changes made by the Nationalist and Communist Parties. Though Chinese opera has never fully recovered from this suppression, it nevertheless remains a vibrant part of China's past and a unique element of its modern culture.

In Chinese opera, the storyline is far more important than the development of complex, realistic, or believable characters. The stage set is either empty or simple and spare. An orchestra of from eight to ten musicians sits to one side. Realistic depictions of time and space are generally ignored. For example, to indicate a long journey, an actor will trace the boundaries of the stage with his footsteps. To illustrate the features of a natural landscape, such as mountains or lakes, the actors will stack boxes or lay cloth on the floor. Dialogue is minimal as well. Elaborate costumes, exaggerated body movements, mime, and colorful face paint help to identify the general qualities of each character. The hero marches across the stage with an upright, determined step. The villain creeps in, his shoulders hunched, his eyes beady. The hero's face is often painted red, symbolizing loyalty and courage, or black, representing righteousness. The villain's face is often painted white, the color of deception.

Twentieth-Century Chinese Music

Western classical and popular music did not reach China until the rise of the New Culture Movement in the 1910s, when a reverence for traditional Chinese culture was largely replaced by an obsession with the West. American and European musicians, brought to the attention of international audiences by radio broadcasts and phonograph records, became very popular. Classical European music and modern American jazz could be heard in many of the concert halls and nightclubs in China's larger cities.

However, as with literature, the government came to view music as an instrument of political revolution and propaganda. Soon, the glories of nationalism and modernization were being sung by school choirs. The rise of nationalism also sparked a revival of Chinese rural folk music, which was celebrated as the true

A group of friends get together in a scenic garden to enjoy each other's folk melodies. Folk music is one of the most popular and beloved styles of music in China and continues to draw the largest audiences.

music of the common man. Under Mao Zedong, these traditional melodies were updated with heavy-handed Communist-themed lyrics.

After the creation of the People's Republic of China in 1949, musicians began to enjoy greatly increased social status and cultural influence. However, as with artists working in other fields, the Chinese Communist Party imposed an ever-increasing degree of censorship on musicians. The Cultural Revolution brought an end to independent musical composition that was free of government oversight. Under the direction of Mao's wife, Jiang Qing, the government chose eight "Revolutionary Model" operas. These pieces, along with songs based on Mao's writings and a few Communist anthems such as "The East Is Red," dominated the musical scene during this time. The eight model operas, with titles such as *The Red Detachment of Women* and *Taking Tiger Mountain by Strategy,* were flat, bland pieces of Communist propaganda that were mostly concerned with a highly sentimental battle between pure good (Communism) and pure evil (capitalism).

Today's Music

With the reforms of the late 1970s came a renewed interest in traditional Chinese music. This trend was short-lived, however, soon to be replaced by an overwhelming interest in the Western genres of rock and pop. Because rock music typically seeks to challenge authority, and pop music tends to celebrate consumer culture, China has not been a breeding ground for these styles of music. Instead, most popular modern music comes to China from the freer societies of Taiwan and Hong Kong, where the Chinese dialect in which the songs are sung—Cantonese—has lent its name to one genre, Canto pop.

Dance

Chinese dance is an ancient art form. Neolithic ceramic pots dating from about 4000 BC show colorful dancing figures along their sides. It is thought that Chinese people from this era engaged in group dances in which the participants locked arms and stamped their feet while singing to instrumental accompaniment. Chinese dancers used movements of the hands and feet to express their respect for the spirits of heaven and Earth, to act out aspects of their everyday life, and to give expression to shared feelings of joy and delight. Dance was also a performing art that brought pleasure to

A procession of Shui women perform a traditional folk dance in Guizhou, China. Guizhou, a southwestern, subtropical region of China, is home to the largest population and greatest variety of ethnic groups in China. Many annual festivals are held to celebrate the customs of each ethnicity.

both the performers and the audience.

Chinese dance can be divided into four main categories: ceremonial (such as praying to the gods for a good harvest), dramatic (to record and celebrate important historical events), martial (to demonstrate fighting techniques), and agricultural (to celebrate nature and farmwork). In nonmilitary dances, dancers held feather banners in their hands, symbolizing the fruits of the day's hunting or fishing. In the large group military dance, dancers carried weapons in their hands and moved forward and backward in coordinated group motion. One dance, the Ten Movement Music dance, incorporated dance elements from China, Korea, India, Persia, and central Asia into one huge production. This dance featured intricate body movements, colorful costumes and props, poetry, songs, and a dramatic plot. It was a predecessor of modern Chinese opera.

Today, ballet and modern dance of the Western world share the stage with traditional Chinese folk dances. In China's new era of greater freedom, dancers and choreographers are experimenting more with dance forms and dancers' bodies. Even as they explore long forbidden Western styles of dance, however, many companies continue to draw on traditional Chinese dance for inspiration. In addition, Chinese folk-dance troupes travel the world and entertain millions of Westerners who are fascinated and dazzled by the ancient and colorful traditions.

FAMOUS FOODS AND RECIPES OF CHINA

9

In China, eating a meal or even a snack can take on cultural and social significance. Enjoying moon cakes, the sweet pastries served during the Full Moon Festival, is a celebration of the passing of time. Family banquets in honor of new births, weddings, funerals, and other occasions are communal events that involve strict and elaborate rituals. Even fast food can have special meaning. Many patrons at the McDonald's restaurant in Beijing, the world's largest branch of the McDonald's chain, say that the experience of eating there is uplifting because it offers them a glimpse of modern, Western life that is still mostly off-limits to them.

Traditional Chinese cuisine is varied and balanced, a perfect blend of yin and yang, the opposing forces that have driven the universe since creation. According to Chinese tradition, foods are either *liang*, meaning "cool," or *re*, meaning "hot." Crab and fruit are examples of the former. Peanuts and oil are examples of the latter. The Chinese long believed that the food a person ate determined his or her mood and behavior. A well-balanced life demanded a well-balanced diet, with equal portions of liang and re. Certain foods were also thought to have the power to heal the sick. "Cool" foods, for example, were said to be able to cure fevers. Although many of these beliefs have fallen out of popular practice, Chinese cuisine remains varied, balanced, and health conscious.

At left, a vegetable seller with her baby strapped to her back prepares for the morning shoppers at a Guizhou market. In the small towns of ethnically diverse Guizhou, people from various ethnic groups and surrounding villages gather every five or six days to buy and sell food and other goods. Above, a street vendor has displayed cold noodles with four different types of soy-based sauce.

Large quantities of fruits and nuts go on sale at the Kashgar Market in Xinjiang. Kashgar boasts one of the most vibrant bazaars in the world.

Fan and *Cai*

A well-balanced Chinese meal is made up of *fan* and *cai*. Fan refers to starches, such as grains, and cai refers to meats, fruits, vegetables, and all of the other ingredients in a dish. Fan is generally considered the more important of the two, and it is sometimes called *zhushi*, or "primary food." Conversely, cai is known as *fushi*, or "secondary food."

Traditionally, rice is the most common form of fan in central and southern China, where the climate and the availability of water create ideal conditions for its cultivation. Its equivalent in the north is millet, a grainy cereal. In modern China, wheat, sorghum, and corn are also popular forms of fan. Rice is eaten whole or ground into flour and prepared as noodles. Wheat, millet, and corn can be eaten whole, prepared as noodles, or used to make the casings for dumplings and cakes. Dumplings, such as *huntun* (wonton) and *jiaozi*, are small pockets of dough that are stuffed with meat, bean curd, or a sweet paste, and then steamed, fried, or boiled. Chinese cakes may be more aptly described as steamed buns.

Cai varies greatly depending on locality. Traditional dishes drew on the crops and livestock available in a particular area. This led to the development of China's many distinctive regional cuisines and specialties.

On the island of Coloane, near Macao, a fisherman puts out dried fish for the early morning market crowds. The city of Macao, a former Portuguese colony, is famous around the world for its fish-curing methods.

Jiaozi: Boiled Dumplings

These Chinese dumplings are especially popular during the Chinese New Year season.

Directions: In a large bowl, dissolve the salt into the cold water. Slowly add the water to the flour, stirring to mix, until it forms a dough, adjusting the amount of water or flour as necessary. Knead the dough into a smooth ball. Cover and let rest for twenty minutes.

While the dough is resting, prepare the filling ingredients. Add the salt, soy sauce, and white pepper to the meat, stirring in only one direction. Add the remaining ingredients and mix well.

To make the dumpling dough: Knead the dough until it forms a smooth ball. Separate into three equal sections. Shape each section into a cylinder approximately 1 inch (2.5 cm) in diameter. Cut each section into twenty equal pieces, scoring the dough if necessary. Roll out each piece into a 3–3.5-inch (7.5–9-cm) circle.

To make the dumplings: Place a small portion of the filling into the middle of each wrapper. Fold the dough over the filling into a half-moon shape and pinch the edges to seal. Continue with the remainder. The recipe should make approximately sixty dumplings.

Jiaozi Dough
3 c. flour
Up to 1¼ c. cold water
¼ tsp. salt

Filling
10.5 ounces fresh Chinese (Napa) cabbage
½ pound ground meat (pork or beef)
1 tsp. salt
1 tbsp. soy sauce
¼ tsp. fresh ground white pepper, or to taste
½ green onion, minced
2 slices fresh ginger, minced
3 tbsp. sesame oil

Bring a large pot of water to a boil. Add half the dumplings, giving them a gentle stir so they don't stick together. Bring the water back to a boil, and add 1/2 cup of cold water. Add the remaining dumplings. Cover and repeat. When the dumplings come to a boil for a third time, they are ready. Drain and remove. If desired, they can be pan-fried at this point. Serve with your favorite soy dipping sauce. Jiaozi can be frozen in a sealed plastic bag and reheated when desired.

(This recipe for Chinese dumplings is adapted from a recipe by Chinese cooking instructor Lucya Lu, published in the *Calgary Herald*, February 18, 1996.)

The Ingredients

An incomplete list of the countless ingredients common in Chinese cooking would include pork, crab, shrimp, sole (a type of fish), eggs, bean curd, bamboo shoots, ginger, celery, cabbage, duck, quail, chicken, bean sprouts, green onions, mushrooms, figs, walnuts, persimmons (berries), and lychee fruit. Perhaps the most famous ingredient in Chinese cooking is soy sauce, a salty, brown liquid that adds flavor and color to countless dishes. Soy sauce was a mainstay of Chinese cooking as early as the tenth century BC, during the Zhou dynasty.

Chinese cooks demand that their ingredients be as fresh as possible. For this reason, people usually shop for groceries every day. In towns and cities across China, fish and produce markets swarm with shoppers stocking up for the day. Pre-packaged ingredients are available, but fresh produce is preferred. However, many dishes, such as pork braised in pickled cabbage or preserved Chinese duck and sausage, do call for ingredients that have been preserved through sugaring, salting, pickling, drying, soaking, or smoking.

While some ingredients are unique to or closely associated with Chinese cooking, most are found in the cooking of many cultures around the world. What distinguishes Chinese cuisine is the way in which these common ingredients are prepared.

Though great importance is placed on the freshness of ingredients in Chinese cooking, they are almost never served raw. Instead, ingredients are first cut into bite-sized morsels, perfect for eating with chopsticks, the slender wooden utensils that first made their appearance at Chinese tables during the Shang dynasty. Next, the ingredients are lightly cooked, most commonly in a large, round-bottomed pan

A kitchen table is cluttered with traditional Chinese ingredients, such as mushrooms, leeks, garlic, and ginger.

called a wok. Usually, the ingredients are deep fried in oil, stir fried (swiftly tossed with a dash of oil), or steamed on racks in a covered wok.

Tea

In China, tea is more than a beverage; it is a social institution. Perhaps originating as far back as the Han dynasty, it became the daily drink of millions of Chinese in the time of the Song. Throughout history, many Chinese have made a ritual of tea, inventing creative and symbolic methods of preparing, serving, and enjoying it. The majority of people, however, simply drink it, often in establishments known as teahouses.

The teahouse achieved the height of its popularity during the nineteenth century. The humblest type of teahouse was simply a business that sold hot water for cooking and bathing. On the side, it also sold tea. More elegant teahouses catered to the well-to-do. Many teahouses provided entertainment in the form of musicians, storytellers, or other performers, free of charge. The teahouse became a kind of local meeting house for friends and colleagues. Over tea, intellectuals shared ideas, businesspeople made deals, and matchmakers tried to arrange marriages between young men and women.

During the early decades of the twentieth century, teahouses fell out of favor and began to disappear. Nationalists criticized the teahouse as old-fashioned and rustic, qualities that were out of step with a society bent on modernization. The Communists abolished almost all private businesses, including teahouses. However, the teahouse has also undergone a twenty-first century revival, appealing primarily to young people by offering sleek and modern décor and free Internet access.

A zig-zagging bridge in Shanghai's Yuyüan Garden leads to a tea-house. The garden includes more than forty scenic spots scattered throughout the grounds.

DAILY LIFE AND CUSTOMS IN CHINA

10

G iven the rigors of a largely agricultural and industrial economy, China's workers historically have not had much time for leisure. In May 1997, however, China officially instituted the five-day workweek. With greater modernization came more leisure time for Chinese workers, as machines began to increase efficiency and save time.

Film and Television

The Chinese enjoy watching television, which draws on every genre of popular American programming—from "news magazines" (like our *60 Minutes* or *Dateline*) to rowdy daytime talk shows to dramatic soap operas—as well as more original, homegrown shows. Movies are also very popular in China. The top-grossing

film in Chinese history is *Titanic*, directed by James Cameron in 1997. The Chinese film industry is very active, but American movies are the most popular and earn the most money. A notable exception is the 1999 Chinese-made film *Be There or Be Square*, directed by Feng Xiaogong, which broke box office records as China's highest-grossing domestic film. Even this film has an American connection, however. It is a romantic comedy about Beijing emigrants living in Los Angeles.

At left, a young woman competes in a martial arts competition. Martial arts have traditionally been used as methods of physical combat, but they can also be practiced to promote emotional and spiritual health. Above, young Chinese girls practice at a gymnastics school in preparation for a national competition in Hangzhou, in Zhejiang Province in southeast China. Young gymnasts hope to be spotted in these competitions and recruited for the Chinese Olympic team.

A scene from the movie *Crouching Tiger, Hidden Dragon* (2000), directed by Taiwanese director Ang Lee. The movie, set in ancient China, was celebrated for its stunningly choreographed and photographed martial arts scenes.

Sports, Martial Arts, and Games

The Chinese enjoy physical activity. Sports familiar to Westerners are also popular in China, particularly gymnastics, swimming, diving, basketball, and baseball. The Chinese are passionate competitors in two sports we consider recreational activities—table tennis (Ping-Pong) and badminton. The Chinese practice a variety of martial arts. Perhaps the most popular is *taijiquan*, known as tai chi chuan, or simply tai chi, by Westerners. Taijiquan is a descendant of traditional Chinese karate that has been transformed, in modern times, to what often looks like slow-motion shadowboxing. The movements are believed to strengthen an individual's *qi*, the vital energy that the Chinese believe flows through all things. Today, taijiquan is practiced primarily by the elderly, who gather together in public spaces in the early morning hours to perform the slow, steady moves in unison.

Another popular activity is *qigong*. Qigong combines meditation, breathing exercises, and gymnastics. Most people who practice it believe it promotes physical and mental health. Some people even believe it can cure serious diseases and allow its most devoted practitioners to tell the future, see through walls, and levitate (float above the ground).

In addition to sports and exercise, the Chinese also enjoy pets. Caged crickets are perhaps the most popular because of the beauty of their songs. Less pleasantly, crickets are also kept to fight against each other as "sport." Cricket fighting became a popular game around AD 900 and continues to this day. Chinese people enjoy more peaceful games, too, including *majiang* (called mah-jong by Westerners), *weiqi*, and *xiangqi*. Majiang is a four-player game similar to dominoes. Weiqi is a game of strategy and conquest played with stones on a grid. Xiangqi is similar to chess.

Shaolin Temple, built in 495, is famous not only as one of China's important Buddhist shrines, but also as the ancient birthplace of the martial art kung fu. Today, Shaolin is still an important kung fu training center.

The One-Child Policy

As we have discussed previously in chapter 5, to ensure the survival of the family line, the inheritance of family property, and security in old age, parents in imperial China were under enormous pressure to produce male children. This was so important that toward the close of the imperial era, it was still legal for a man to divorce his wife if she failed to produce a son.

Since the imperial era, China's population has been growing so fast that there is no longer enough farmland to support it. Today, China boasts the world's largest population, around 1.3 billion. The country covers an area slightly larger than the United States, but the vast majority of this land cannot support large-scale agriculture.

In the early 1980s, the government launched a campaign to slow population growth by allowing every couple only one child. The policy has had mixed results. The responsibility of

A group of Chinese children play Ping-Pong. In China, Ping-Pong is not just a recreational sport but is played competitively at the national and international level. It is one of the featured sports in the summer Olympic Games.

A poster promotes China's one-child policy, which encourages families to use birth control and have only one child in order to control population growth.

enforcement has been placed in the hands of local bureaucrats. In rural areas, many communities have adopted a two-child policy, while many other communities ignore the government's order altogether. Many rural families have found it relatively easy to bribe authorities to create false documents that conceal the true number of children a family has. In cities, authorities have been stricter in enforcing the policy, and birth rates have gone down substantially.

Other factors have contributed to making the average Chinese family smaller than it once was. As has been the case throughout world history, wealthier and better-educated communities tend to produce fewer children. Wealthy parents do not need the free labor that children can provide on the family farm. When they become elderly, they can pay for home care or visiting nurses, rather than rely on their children to look

after them. Today, many potential parents believe that children simply cost too much. The variety of expensive entertainment geared toward the young, tuition for sixteen or more years of education, ever more elaborate wedding

A photograph of a one-child family from Xian, China. The one-child policy was introduced in 1979 and is credited with preventing 250 million births since 1980. Even with the policy, China's population is expected to increase from 1.3 billion in 2003 to 1.6 billion in 2050.

Mao Zedong's Little Red Book is a collection of speeches and quotes that has approximately 5 billion copies in print in several languages, making it one of the largest print-runs in publishing history.

ceremonies—these all contribute to the high cost of raising children.

A Changing Economy, A Changing Society

Though the Communist Party has eased restrictions on China's economy and moved the country closer to a free market, the party still resists embracing all-out capitalism and Western influences. Though it has initiated countless economic reforms aimed at raising the overall standard of living, the Communist Party remains on guard against what it calls "bourgeois liberalism," which basically includes any ideas that do not express the principles of Communist revolution. "Bourgeois liberalism" is often a code phrase for Western influences. As a result, experimental literature, popular music, cinema, and even fast food are often labeled in this way and condemned.

A growing nationalist, anti-Western movement has gained significant popular support recently. T-shirts and playing cards bearing Mao Zedong's portrait and rock songs set to lyrics taken from his writings have become popular across the country. Many people, perhaps weary from decades of economic change and political corruption and repression, appear to be genuinely nostalgic for the Maoist era. They may only be craving the social stability that an iron-fisted ruler provides. Or perhaps they are frustrated with the current state of affairs. But just as capitalism has begun to take hold, many Chinese find themselves looking back fondly on a very dark chapter in China's history.

EDUCATION AND WORK IN CHINA

11

E ducation is a central aspect of Chinese culture. In China, teaching has always been at the heart of philosophy, the arts, political discussion, and entertainment. However, academic curiosity has not always been supported by intellectual freedom—the freedom to explore subjects, discuss issues, and state opinions without fear of punishment. During periods when academic freedom was suppressed, China's educational system became sterile and neglected as students learned only what the government wanted them to know and believe. Today, China has embraced both the nation's long historical tradition of scholarship and a modern, secular approach to learning.

Rujia

At the heart of classical education in China lies the Confucian doctrine, known as *rujia*, the "teaching of the learned." Rujia is a belief in tradition, patience, obedience, and social hierarchy. Confucius sought to create just and fair-minded rulers in a time when righteous leaders were scarce and China was in a state of political chaos. As we have seen, education was believed to be the means by which the Confucian ideal was achieved. Only the educated man could achieve the state of junzi and become the "superior man."

At left, a young Chinese boy copies his homework on the blackboard at a Guangzhou elementary school. Elementary school children in China study drawing, music, mathematics, reading, and history. In third grade students begin to learn a second language, which is usually English. Above, an eighteenth-century painting depicts a traditional Confucian classroom.

This scroll depicts Chinese students taking a civil service exam. The Chinese civil service exams began around the sixth century BC. They were designed to prepare students to serve in the emperor's government. By AD 115, students were being tested in the six arts: music, archery, horsemanship, arithmetic, writing, and knowledge of the rituals and ceremonies of both public and private life.

Confucian philosophy had a profound effect on Chinese attitudes toward education throughout the country's imperial age. The philosophy appealed to the ruling classes because it supported the rule of the emperor and gave great honor to the scholar elite. Many emperors hoped to use Confucian thought to standardize Chinese education and culture. Yet there was no formalized schooling in the early imperial era. From the smallest rural villages to the emperor's lavish court, young men were individually tutored in the Confucian classics, which made up the foundation of knowledge tested in the civil service examinations. Civil service exams were open to all applicants, regardless of class. An average of 280 successful candidates per year were given government posts and enjoyed very high social status.

As early as 124 BC, Emperor Han Wudi founded an imperial university where a thorough Confucian education was offered free of charge. A century later, the university had some 3,000 students. After another hundred years, the student body had grown to 50,000. Other imperial universities followed, perhaps the most famous being Hanlin Yüan, founded in the eighth century AD.

The Beginning of a Revolution

In the final years of the nineteenth century, as imperial rule fell into decline, a group of Confucian scholars argued for major changes within Chinese society. These included proposals for the creation of a constitutional monarchy and a parliament to replace the current imperial dictatorship. In a constitutional monarchy, a king or queen rules the land, but his or her power is limited and controlled by the nation's constitution and sometimes by a parliament filled with representatives of the people. Kang Yu Wei was a prominent member of this revolutionary movement who argued

Political and social reformer Kang Yu Wei was a strong supporter of Confucianism and reform of the civil service exams. Through Kang's influence and urging, Emperor Kuang-hsu founded Beijing University.

that Confucius himself was an innovative thinker and that he would have supported major social change in response to modern problems.

In the final years of the Qing dynasty, the emperor agreed to rebuild the government as a constitutional monarchy. Significant educational reforms were also made. In 1904, a national system of primary (elementary), secondary (middle school), and high schools was created. The following year, the civil service examinations were abolished. In addition, the government encouraged students to study overseas, particularly in Japan. These reforms undermined the authority of the traditional scholar-elite bureaucracy. Education was available to all, not just those hoping to enter the civil service. This brought increased social mobility (the ability to move up in class) and intellectual freedom. However, it was not until 1907 that the government officially supported education for girls. Even then, girls could only enroll in all-girl primary schools and teacher-training institutions. Women were finally granted the right to attend secondary school in 1912 and the right to enroll in high school in 1919.

The modern school system became the center of an aggressive youth movement. Students frequently led protests, went on strike, and published journals to voice their opposition to school policies and national affairs. Students returning from overseas study—by 1906 some 9,000 Chinese students were studying in Japan alone—raised their voices in revolt, too. They had experienced more free and open societies while abroad and returned with a desire to bring about change in China.

Education and Maoist Thought

The Chinese Communist Party stressed the importance of creating citizens who could read and write. Party leaders believed that only an educated population could wage a national class struggle and overthrow the ruling elite. Even before coming to power in

Members of the Red Guard line up in front of a photograph of Mao Zedong during a ceremony in Peking (now Beijing) in 1966. Members of the Red Guard were usually young, single-minded teenagers, enlisted by Mao to enforce hard-line Communist ideals throughout China.

1949, the party established rural schools to promote literacy and teach useful skills. Once it gained power, the Communist Party's educational system incorporated kindergarten, primary school, junior and senior high school, and university-level institutions. It had direct control over all these schools and what could and could not be taught in them.

Education, particularly during the Great Leap Forward of the 1950s, was heavily influenced by China's Communist neighbor and mentor, the Soviet Union. Many Chinese students were sent to study in the Soviet Union, and the Soviet Union sent textbooks and technical manuals to China. Translations of these texts made up the core reading materials of many schools. The curriculum emphasized the combining of physical and intellectual pursuits. However, all intellectual activity was severely restricted by Communist ideology. Agricultural communes funded work-study schools where urban university students and intellectuals would be sent (often against their will) to perform manual labor alongside peasants.

When the Great Leap Forward formally ended in 1960, the Communist Party, in the hands of Mao's designated successors, Deng Xiaoping and Liu Shaoqi, turned away from Mao's political

A schoolgirl wears a Red Guard button on her jacket, signaling her membership in the group. For many young Chinese, joining the Red Guard meant gaining a political role and a sense of importance in the development of the new Maoist China.

and social policies. In reforming the educational system, the party closed the rural work-study schools and redirected the focus of education away from cultivating "redness" (or a commitment to Communist ideology) and toward creating experts in each academic field. Classroom instruction became more important than laboring in the fields. Mao, though no longer head of the Communist Party, was still supreme commander of the nation and army. Angered by the new reforms, he responded by launching the Great Proletarian Cultural Revolution.

The Cultural Revolution was a war waged on institutions of authority, and Mao chose the young students of the Red Guard as his foot soldiers in this campaign. In the summer of 1966, schools were shut down. Freed from the responsibility of going to classes, Red Guards roamed the countryside, committing acts of vandalism and violence wherever they went. Mao finally ordered the People's Liberation Army to suppress the Red Guard revolts in 1967, though this brutal era would not come to a final end until 1976 with Mao's death and Deng's return to power. Schools were reopened, but college-level entrance exams were done away with. Instead, students were recommended by their work unit and required to perform manual labor before enrolling in college.

Education in China Today

Following the end of the Red Guard revolts and Deng Xiaoping's reforms of the late 1970s, Mao's destructive policies came to an end. A modern, Western-style educational system focused on producing academics, not political activists, was put into

Today, Chinese children begin computer classes between the ages of six and ten. At a primary school in rural China, young students are learning how to type, surf the Internet, and use basic software.

place. The manual labor requirement was abolished. Nationwide standardized tests were given, and college-level curricula were developed.

Despite the government's regaining control of the schools, Chinese academic institutions have remained centers for lively discussion, debate, and discord. The demonstrations of the middle and late 1980s, culminating in the Tian'anmen Square demonstration of 1989, were led by university students and their teachers. These demonstrators voiced their unhappiness with Chinese society, Communist Party rule, and, more specifically, with the state of education in China. The protesters argued that many of China's institutions of higher learning lacked adequate facilities, challenging coursework, and opportunities for career advancement.

China's education woes are serious indeed. Since the late 1970s, some 300,000 Chinese have studied abroad, hoping to find educational and economic opportunities overseas that they could not find at home. Of these, only about 100,000 students have returned to China. Furthermore, a study conducted in 1990 found that roughly 27 percent of Chinese women and 10 percent of men ages 16 to 65 had never been to school. Less than 35 percent of women had completed middle school, compared to around 50 percent of men. Finally, a scant 3 percent of men and 1.7 percent of women had completed college. These statistics suggest that most Chinese do not have access to any but the most basic education. They also point out a great divide between the educational opportunities enjoyed by men and those granted to women. Similar inequalities exist between rural and urban students because most of China's education budget goes to urban schools.

Work and Industry

In the late 1970s, the Communist Party began to relax its control over China's economy, allow foreign investment, and let market forces determine prices and supplies of goods and services. In addition, the old Communist policy of land collectivization ended, allowing individual households to farm and make money off their land. Under this policy of economic liberalization, China's gross domestic product (GDP) quadrupled between 1978 and 1998. Both agriculture and manufacturing industries have seen large increases in production.

More than half of the Chinese population is involved in agriculture, even though only about 10 percent of the nation's land can be cultivated, mostly in the east. The remainder of the land is too rough and rocky, dry, or mountainous. Agriculture

A long line of workers carry heavy bags of coal from the mines to waiting barges in Fengjie, in China's East Sichuan Province. The coal will eventually be delivered to power plants. China has the largest mining industry in the world, but it is also one of the least safe. The total number of coal mine-related deaths in 2001 was 5,395.

accounts for 15.2 percent of China's GDP. China is the largest producer of rice, wheat, cotton, and tobacco. It is a major producer of sweet potatoes, sorghum, millet, barley, peanuts, corn, soybeans, potatoes, silk, tea, sugarcane, and sugar beets. It is the world's largest producer of red meat, while fish and pork provide the main source of protein in the Chinese diet. China's huge agricultural industry, including livestock, allows it to be self-sufficient in terms of food. It can grow or produce all the grains, meat, fish, dairy products, eggs, fruit, and vegetables it needs without having to import anything from other countries.

China is one of the world's most important mineral-producing countries, ranking first in coal production. Iron, oil, tin, salt, and mercury are also major export industries. Heavy industries, such as iron and steel manufacturing, thrive throughout the country, as do brick, tile, cement, and food processing plants. Light industries began to develop in the late 1970s, after the creation of "special economic zones" designed to attract foreign investment. Some of these industries include

Chinese engineers manufacture integrated circuits, or chips. These are used in a variety of devices, including microprocessors, audio and video equipment, and automobiles. About half of China's workforce is employed in agriculture, but industry has begun to thrive with the opening of the economy to Western investment. Many Chinese citizens now have jobs in textile, toy, automobile, and electronics companies.

consumer goods, toys, plastics, textiles, clothing, chemical fertilizers, building materials, machinery, electronics, and weapons systems.

Given all this recent economic growth and activity, it can be hoped that China's chronically high unemployment rate (10 percent in urban areas) will begin to come down. Many Chinese workers are underemployed, meaning they can often find only part-time and low-paying work. From 60 to 100 million rural workers travel back and forth between villages and the cities, piecing together a meager living from a series of part-time jobs.

The Future of China

On three separate occasions in the twentieth century, the people of China have embarked on a revolutionary course to dramatically change their society. First came the

An enormous housing project rises high above Hong Kong. In a region with a population of more than 7 million, where open land is scarce and expensive, building upward is a more economical and realistic solution to the housing crunch than is building outward. Many of Hong Kong's residents live in high-rise apartment buildings, some of which are more than seventy floors tall.

fall of the Qing dynasty and the end of imperial China at the hands of the Nationalists in 1911. Next came the Communist revolt against the Nationalist republic in 1949. Finally, the Chinese Communist Party was revived under the reform-minded leaders of the late 1970s, who transformed China into a vibrant socialist market economy. Today, China is still recovering from the economic crisis that gripped Asia at the turn of the twenty-first century. Ethnic tensions in the country's autonomous regions have reached a fever pitch. The outcome of the "one country, two systems" policy toward Hong Kong remains to be seen. Under this policy, Hong Kong exists under Chinese rule but is allowed to govern itself democratically and operate a capitalist economy. China continues to be condemned worldwide for its occupation of Tibet. Western culture has taken a firm hold of the nation's youth, who seem to have abandoned political resistance and protest in favor of pop music. In short, China is a nation in flux whose future looks uncertain but filled with potential.

CHINA
AT A GLANCE

HISTORY

The Xia dynasty is traditionally believed to be China's first civilization, but whether or not it actually existed is not known for sure. There is no clear and convincing archaeological evidence to support the legends of Yu, the dynasty's founder, or any of his successors. The Shang (1766–1122 BC), later known as the Yin, is the first dynasty for which a definite archaeological record exists. The succeeding dynasties were, in order, Zhou (1122–256 BC), Qin (221–206 BC), Han (206 BC–AD 220), the Six Dynasties (220–589), Sui (589–618), Tang (618–907), the Five Dynasties (907–960), Song (960–1279), Yüan (1279–1368), Ming (1368–1644), and Qing (1644–1912).

During the Qing dynasty, China came under the influence and colonial control of the major foreign powers, including Great Britain, the United States, Germany, and Japan. Mass revolt broke out in protest against the government's inability to stem the rising tide of foreign occupation. Local leaders from the southern provinces announced the creation of an independent republic with Sun Yat-sen, the leader of a Nationalist revolutionary group called the Guomindang, as its president. In February 1912, Yüan Shikai negotiated the abdication (stepping down) of the dynasty. For his role in the revolution, Yüan was given the office of president of the new Republic of China.

Yüan Shikai was a corrupt and inefficient president who did not appreciate or value the aims of the Nationalist revolution. Urban intellectuals under the leadership of Mao Zedong formed the Communist Party and led the protest against Yüan. When Yüan died, control of the government fell to the hands of various military authorities. In 1949, the Communist Party waged a long campaign against the scattered Nationalist government, won, and declared the creation of the People's Republic of China.

The Chinese Communist Party sought to dramatically change the basic structure of Chinese society by putting an end to private land ownership, sparking

Thousands of student protesters gather in Tian'anmen Square on May 4, 1989, to demand greater freedom of speech and democracy.

class struggle, and promoting a kind of socialism in which government owns all businesses and industries and private property is outlawed. These goals were realized during Mao Zedong's long rule of China in the abolition of private ownership and the creation of the commune system of the 1950s; the Great Leap Forward, begun in 1958; and the Cultural Revolution, begun in 1966. In 1976, Mao died, and the Chinese Communist Party began the long process of reforming China. Private ownership was restored, foreign investment was encouraged, and new freedoms were extended to the Chinese people.

However, this "reform" government was also plagued by corruption, and the youth of China rose up in revolt once again. These demonstrations culminated in the Tian'anmen Square protests of 1989, which the government suppressed with deadly force. Today, China's students face the same social and political problems that angered the activists of a generation ago. It remains to be seen if they, too, will risk their lives by raising their voices in protest and if that protest will lead to a new era of greater freedom in China.

ECONOMY

The reforms of the late 1970s brought dramatic improvements to China's economy and to the standard of living for most Chinese people. Today, China is a socialist market economy. This means that it trades with other nations and allows consumer demand to determine what products get made and sold and at what price. Yet China's government still regulates the nation's economy to a greater degree than most Western governments do by trying to exert some control over prices and supplies and by promoting Chinese products over imported goods.

Billions of dollars are contributed to China's economy by foreign business each year. Tourism, banking, finance, and real estate form the backbone of China's coastal urban economies, where the greatest proportion of China's population lives. However, agriculture is still widespread and central to the economies of the central and southern provinces. The gross domestic product (the total amount of goods and services produced in a year) has quadrupled since 1978. However, in 2002, the average per capita (per person) income was still only $4,400.

GOVERNMENT AND POLITICS

In theory, China's government is driven by the people, who elect deputies to represent them in the National People's Congress and the local people's congresses. Since China has only one political party, the Communist Party, that is allowed to hold power, there is no true choice of candidates. The Chinese president is the head of state. The head of state announces the laws that are made by the Congress, appoints diplomats and members of the State Council, hosts foreign dignitaries, and ratifies (approves) treaties.

The State Council is the highest administrative body in the Chinese government. It includes appointed officials in the positions of state councillors, premier, vice premier, secretary-general, and ministers of foreign affairs, defense, education, and so on. Members of the State Council create and

Deputies stand at the conclusion of the sixteenth Communist Party Congress, held in the Great Hall of the People in November 2002.

enforce administrative policies for the government. The Central Military Commission commands all armed forces, including the army, the police, and the reserve. The judicial system is made up of the basic people's courts, intermediate people's courts, and the Supreme People's Court. Finally, there are "procuratorial" bodies at the state and local levels, which serve as supervisors over all administrative and legal matters within the court system. The Chinese Communist Party, with some 63 million members, is the only political party in power. There are eight other recognized political parties, and representatives of these groups can express their views in political conferences and forums at the invitation of the Communist Party.

TIMELINE

500,000 BC

Homo erectus "Peking Man" lives and dies in what will become northern China.

5000– 2500 BC

Painted pottery is made.

Shang Dynasty

1766–1122 BC

The first Chinese dynasty for which historical records exist. The first appearance of Chinese written characters.

Eastern Zhou Dynasty

551 BC

Confucius is born. Siddhartha Gautama, the founder of Buddhism, lives in India at about the same time.

Qin Dynasty

221–202 BC

Emperor Qin Shi Huangdi unifies China. Regional defensive walls are linked together to form the Great Wall.

Han Dynasty

206 BC–AD 220

Confucius's teachings become the basis of Chinese thought and the civil service. Buddhism is brought to China from India. Paper is invented.

Ming Dynasty

1368–1644

Chinese drive Mongols out of China. Construction of the Forbidden City begins.

Qing Dynasty

1644

The Ming are conquered by nomads from Manchuria. China is again ruled by foreigners.

1840

The First Opium War between China and Britain begins.

1842

The British win the Opium War and force China to hand over control of many of its ports, including Hong Kong. Anti-foreign sentiment grows.

1894

The First Sino-Japanese War begins as China fights to defend Korean independence against a Japanese invasion.

1896–1900

With the support of the empress, a group of rural marauders known as Boxers begin stirring up anti-Christian anger and attack foreigners. Foreign powers eventually quash the Boxer Rebellion.

1951

China occupies Tibet.

1958

Mao's Great Leap Forward begins.

1966

Mao launches his Cultural Revolution and inspires the youthful Red Guard to attack all symbols and representations of tradition. Mao's Little Red Book is published.

1972

Richard Nixon becomes the first U.S. president to visit China.

1976

Mao Zedong dies.

1978

Chinese economic reforms begin.

Three Kingdoms Era

AD 220–280

The "one Emperor over China" idea is reinforced, eventually cementing imperial authority.

Sui Dynasty

389–618

China is reunified after more than 300 years of fighting. The Great Wall is fortified. The longest human-made river in the world—the Grand Canal—is finished.

Tang Dynasty

618–907

Art, literature, philosophy, and music flourish. The oldest surviving printed book is published in 868. Christian missionaries arrive in China.

Song Dynasty

969–1279

Movable type printing is invented.

Yüan Dynasty

1279–1368

Kublai Khan, the grandson of Mongol conqueror Genghis Khan, overthrows the Song and establishes the Yüan dynasty. This is the first time that China has been ruled by outsiders. China begins commercial and cultural exchanges with the outside world. The Beijing Opera is established.

Republic of China

1911

Sun Yat-sen and his Nationalist Party overthrow the Qing and establish the Republic of China, ending almost 4,000 years of imperial rule.

1921

The Communist Party of China is founded.

1927

The Communists and Nationalists begin fighting each other for control over China.

1937–1945

The Second Sino-Japanese War is waged after Japan invades and brutally attacks China. The conflict will be absorbed by WWII and end after the 1945 U.S. bombing of the Japanese cities of Nagasaki and Hiroshima. At the war's end, the Communists and Nationalists begin fighting again.

People's Republic of China

1949

The Communists, under Mao Zedong, defeat the Nationalists and rename the country the People's Republic of China. The Nationalists, led by Chiang Kai-shek, flee to Taiwan, which they call the Republic of China.

1979

The United States and China establish full diplomatic relations.

1989

Tian'anmen Square protests lead to violent crackdown.

1990

China's first McDonald's restaurant opens.

1997

Britain transfers control of Hong Kong to China. Deng Xiaoping dies.

2003

China's first manned spacecraft successfully returns to Earth after orbiting the planet fourteen times.

CHINA

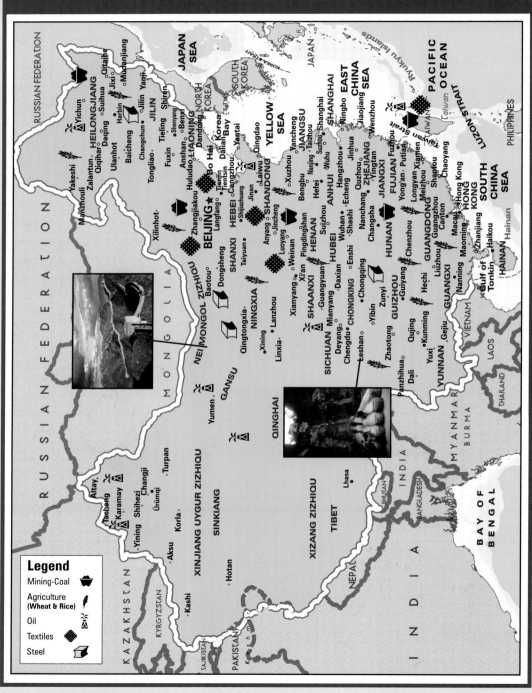

Legend

Mining-Coal

Agriculture
(Wheat & Rice)

Oil

Textiles

Steel

ECONOMIC FACT SHEET

GDP in US$: $5.99 trillion

GDP Sectors: Agriculture 15.2%, industry and construction 51.2%, services 33.6%

Land Use: Arable land 13.31%, permanent crops 1.2%, other 85.49%

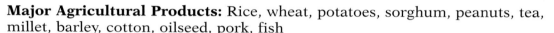

Currency: Yüan: 8.277 yüan to the U.S. dollar

Workforce: Agriculture 50%, industry 22%, services 28%

Major Agricultural Products: Rice, wheat, potatoes, sorghum, peanuts, tea, millet, barley, cotton, oilseed, pork, fish

Major Exports: Machinery and equipment, textiles and clothing, footwear, toys and sporting goods, mineral fuels

Major Imports: Machinery and equipment, mineral fuels, plastics, iron and steel, chemicals

Significant Trading Partners:

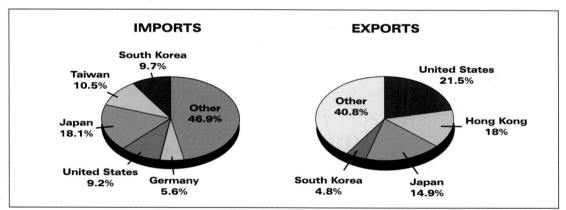

IMPORTS

- South Korea 9.7%
- Taiwan 10.5%
- Japan 18.1%
- United States 9.2%
- Germany 5.6%
- Other 46.9%

EXPORTS

- United States 21.5%
- Hong Kong 18%
- Japan 14.9%
- South Korea 4.8%
- Other 40.8%

Rate of Unemployment: Urban unemployment roughly 10%; substantial unemployment and underemployment in rural areas

Highways: Total: 869,920 miles (1.4 million km)

Railroads: Total 44,490 miles (71,600 km)

Waterways: Total 68,350 miles (110,000 km)

Airports: 500

POLITICAL FACT SHEET

Official Country Name:
People's Republic of China
Capital: Beijing
System of Government:
Communist Republic
Federal Structure:
President and vice president
are elected by the National
People's Congress. A premier
is appointed by the president
and confirmed by the
National People's Congress.

Government Structure: The
unicameral (one house) National People's Congress has 2,985 members elected by municipal, regional, and provincial people's congresses for five-year terms. Judges are appointed to the Supreme People's Court by the National People's Congress.

National Anthem: The music for this anthem was composed by Nieh Erh in 1932, one year after the Japanese invasion of Manchuria, and was dedicated to the volunteers who rose to defend the nation. In 1934, Nieh Erh went to continue his musical studies in Japan, where he was murdered at the age of twenty-four. His song was adopted as the national anthem of the People's Republic of China in 1949. The lyrics are by Tian Han.

Administrative divisions: Twenty-three provinces (Anhui, Fujian, Gansu, Guangdong, Guizhou, Hainan, Hebei, Heilongjiang, Henan, Hubei, Hunan, Jiangsu, Jiangxi, Jilin, Liaoning, Qinghai, Shaanxi, Shandong, Shanxi, Sichuan, Taiwan, Yunnan, and Zhejiang). Five autonomous regions (Guangxi, Inner Mongolia, Ningxia, Tibet, and Xinjiang). Four municipalities (Beijing, Chongqing, Shanghai, and Tianjin). Two special administrative regions (Hong Kong and Macau).

Independence: Qing dynasty replaced by the Republic of China on February 12, 1912. The People's Republic of China established on October 1, 1949.

Constitution: December 4, 1982 (most recent version)

Legal System: Mixture of custom and statute. The legal code, made up largely of criminal law, was instituted in 1980.

Suffrage: Eighteen years of age; universal
Population: 1,286,975,468

CULTURAL FACT SHEET

Official Languages: Standard Chinese or Mandarin (Putonghua, based on the Beijing dialect), Yue (Cantonese), Wu (Shanghaiese), Minbei (Fuzhou), Minnan (Hokkien-Taiwanese), Xiang, Gan, Hakka dialects, minority languages

Major Religions: Taoist, Buddhist, Christian 3–4%, Muslim 1–2 %

Ethnic Groups: Han Chinese 91.9%; Zhuang, Uygur, Hui, Yi, Tibetan, Miao, Manchu, Mongol, Buyi, Korean, and other nationalities 8.1%

Life Expectancy: 72.22 years

Time: Beijing is Greenwich mean time + 8 hours

Literacy Rate: 86% (male: 92.9%, female: 78.8%)

National Flower: Tree peony (unofficial)

National Bird: Crested ibis (unofficial)

Cultural Leaders:

Visual Arts: Fang Li Jun, Liao Bang Ming, Wang Bo, Xhang Xiaogang, Xie Feng, Xue Song, Yu Bo Gang, Zhu Ming

Literature: Ba Jin, Chen Cun, Gao Xingjian, Li Rui, Li Xiao, Mo Yan, Su Tong, Wang Meng, Wang Xiangfu

Entertainment: Ah Nian, Chen Kaige, Jet Li, Jing Yan, Maggie Cheung, Wang Quanan, Wu Ziniu

Sports: Fu Mingxia (diving), Ji Xinpeng (badminton), Kong Linghui (table tennis), Li Xiaopeng (gymnastics), Sun Wen (soccer), Wang Nan (table tennis), Xiong Ni (diving), Yao Ming (basketball)

National Holidays and Festivals

January 1: **New Year's Day**

January 15: **Deng jie—Feast of Lanterns, a new year's celebration**

Late January–early February: **Guonian—Spring Festival**

March 8: **International Women's Day**

March 12: **Arbor Day**

April 4 or 5: **Qingming jie—Festival of Pure Brightness, an ancestor worship festival**

May 1: **International Labor Day**

May 4: **Youth Day**

June 1: **International Children's Day**

July 1: **Anniversary of the Founding of the Chinese Communist Party**

August 1: **Army Day**

September 10: **Teachers' Day**

Late September: **Zhongqiu—Mid-Autumn Festival or Full Moon Festival, a harvest celebration**

October 1: **National Day**

GLOSSARY

autonomy (aw-TAH-nuh-mee) The right or ability to be self-governing.

bureaucracy (byuh-RAH-kruh-see) A government's policy-administering group.

bureaucrat (BYUR-uh-krat) A member of the bureaucracy responsible for administering government policy and programs.

civil service (SIH-vul SUR-vis) The part of a government that administers or enforces its policies and programs.

collectivization (kuh-lek-tih-vih-ZAY-shun) The placing of all private property under the control of a group or government.

communist (KAHM-yuh-nist) A member of a party or movement that argues for the end of private property in favor of the sharing of all goods and wealth.

corrupt (kuh-RUPT) Something that is rotten or bad.

cosmology (kahz-MAH-luh-jee) A theory of the natural order of the universe.

dialect (DY-uh-lekt) A regional variation of a language that may feature different vocabulary, pronunciation, and grammar than other versions of the same language.

dynasty (DY-nuh-stee) A series of rulers who come from the same family or group.

enlightenment (en-LY-ten-ment) A state in which one desires nothing and feels no suffering.

genre (ZHAHN-ruh) A category of artistic, musical, or literary creation distinguished by a particular style, form, or content.

hierarchy (HY-er-ar-kee) The organization of a government, society, family, etc., by a series of rankings, from those with the most power and authority down to those with the least.

imperialism (im-PEER-ee-uh-lih-zum) The practice of gaining power over another nation by seizing its territory or gaining control of its political or economic life.

monsoon (mahn-SOON) A strong wind that periodically blows in the Indian Ocean and southern Asia.

nationalist (NASH-ih-nuh-list) A member of a group that argues for a country's independence and distinct identity.

nomadic (noh-MA-dik) Roaming from place to place with no permanent home.

proletarian (proh-luh-TAYR-ee-un) A member of the lowest social or economic class; the working class.

propaganda (prah-puh-GAN-duh) Ideas and information spread to further one's own cause or harm the cause of an enemy or competitor.

transliteration (trans-lih-tuh-RAY-shun) The spelling of a word from one language using the alphabet of another.

vernacular (ver-NAH-kyuh-lur) The common language of a region or country (as opposed to a literary, formal, or foreign language).

FOR MORE INFORMATION

Asia-Pacific Foundation of Canada
666-999 Canada Place
Vancouver, BC, Canada V6C 3E1
(604) 684-5986
Web site: http://www.asiapacific.ca

Asia Society and Museum
725 Park Avenue
New York, NY 10021
(212) 288-6400
Web site: http://www.asiasociety.org

Association for Asian Studies
1021 East Huron Street
Ann Arbor, MI 48104
(734) 665-2490
Web site: http://www.aasianst.org

Center for Chinese Studies
University of California, Berkeley
2223 Fulton Street, #2328
Berkeley, CA 94720-2328
(510) 643-6321
Web site: http://ieas.berkeley.edu/ccs

Chinese Embassy in the United States
2300 Connecticut Avenue NW
Washington, DC 20008
(202) 328-2500
Web site: http://www.chinaembassy.
  org

Web Sites

Due to the changing nature of Internet links, the Rosen Publishing Group, Inc., has developed an online list of Web sites related to the subject of this book. This site is updated regularly. Please use this link to access the list:

http://www.rosenlinks.com/pswc/chin

FOR FURTHER READING

Beshore, George W. *Science in Ancient China.* New York: Franklin Watts, 1998.

Birch, Cyril. *Tales from China.* New York: Oxford University Press Children's Books, 2000.

Cotterell, Arthur. *Eyewitness: Ancient China.* New York: DK Books, 2000.

Demi. *The Dragon's Tale and Other Animal Fables of the Chinese Zodiac.* New York: Henry Holt & Company, Inc., 1996.

Hall, Eleanor J. *Ancient Chinese Dynasties.* San Diego, CA: Lucent Books, 2000.

Roberts, Moss, ed. *Chinese Fairy Tales and Fantasies.* New York: Pantheon Books, 1980.

Simonds, Nina, Leslie Swartz, and the Children's Museum, Boston. *Moonbeams, Dumplings, and Dragon Boats: A Treasury of Chinese Holiday Tales, Activities, and Recipes.* Fairbanks, AK: Gulliver Books, 2002.

Sis, Peter. *Tibet: Through the Red Box.* New York: Farrar Straus & Giroux, 1998.

Williams, Suzanne, and Andrea Fong. *Made in China: Ideas and Inventions from Ancient China.* Berkeley, CA: Pacific View Press, 1997.

BIBLIOGRAPHY

Bailey, Paul J. *China in the Twentieth Century.* Oxford, England: Blackwell Publishers, 2001.

Creel, Herrle Glessner. *The Birth of China: A Survey of the Formative Period of the Chinese Civilization.* New York: Frederick Ungar Publishing Co., 1954.

Gunde, Richard. *Culture and Customs of China.* Westport, CT: Greenwood Press, 2002.

Haw, Stephen G. *A Traveller's History of China.* New York: Interlink Books, 1995.

Meyer, Milton W. *China: A Concise History.* Lanham, MD: Littlefield Adams, 1994.

Scott, Adolphe Clarence. *Literature and the Arts in Twentieth Century China.* Westport, CT: Greenwood Publishing Group, 1982.

Sickman, Laurence, and Alexander Soper. *The Art and Architecture of China.* New Haven, CT: Yale University Press, 1992.

Tregear, Mary. *Chinese Art.* New York: Thames and Hudson, 1997.

PRIMARY SOURCE IMAGE LIST

Page 20: A fish spear and arrowhead from the late fourth or third millennium BC, excavated at Wu-Chiang, Kiang-Shu, China. Housed in the National Museum, Beijing.

Page 21: A jade ring from the Shang dynasty made sometime between 1500 and 1050 BC. Housed in the British Museum.

Page 22 (bottom): The c. seventh-century AD Buddhist retreat of Bezeklik carved out loess, or compacted dust, near the Gobi Desert along the Silk Road.

Page 23: The Nanking Treaty of Peace, Friendship, Commerce, and Indemnity, signed on August 29, 1842, that ended the three-year Opium War between China and Britain.

Page 24: A late nineteenth-century photograph of rebellious Boxers standing in firing formation.

Page 25: A Keystone View Company photograph taken on December 13, 1919, of accused Boxers kneeling before the Chinese High Court.

Page 26 (top): A c. 1920 photograph of Sun Yat-sen.

Page 26 (bottom): A c. 1910 photograph of Chiang Kai-shek.

Page 27 (top): A 1925 photograph of Mao Zedong.

Page 27 (bottom): An Associated Press photograph of Japanese infantrymen attacking Peking on August 19, 1937, during the Second Sino-Japanese War.

Page 28: A 1949 propaganda poster entitled "People from the Rivers and Mountains."

Page 29: A 1958 photograph by Henri Cartier-Bresson entitled "The 'Great Leap Forward.'"

Page 30: A c. 1966–1967 photograph of Red Guards plastering the walls of Peking University with propaganda posters.

Page 31: A propaganda poster from the Chinese Cultural Revolution, 1966–1976, entitled "Reporting Our Harvest to Chairman Mao." By the Chinese School.

Page 32: A 1984 photograph by AFP Photo of Deng Xiaoping during a visit to the Shenzhen Special Economic Zone.

Page 33: A 1989 photograph by Stuart Franklin of a protester standing before a line of tanks in Tian'anmen Square.

Page 34: A May 18, 1989, photograph by Patrick Zachmann of protesters converging on Tian'anmen Square.

Page 38: This illustrated ink on parchment text is a page from a c. seventh-century sutra entitled *Ten Kings of the World*, found in Dunhuang, China. Housed in the British Library, London, England.

Page 44: A nineteenth-century French engraving of the Ancestral Gods of Medicine. Housed in the Bibliotheque Nationale, Paris, France.

Page 45: An eighteenth-century hand-colored engraving by Pierre Duflos of the Sage King Yu.

Page 46: An 1820 manuscript drawing by Tian-gong Yuan entitled "Pangu Kaitian Pidi" ("Pangu Creating the World"). Located in the Chinese Rare Book Collection, Asian Division, of the Library of Congress, Washington, DC.

Page 48: An 1895 woodblock print of the kitchen god with lunar calendar. Located in the Oriental Museum, Durham University, England.

Page 56: The Feng-Hsien Temple in Longmen, China.

Page 58 (top): A Tang dynasty (618–907) portrait of Confucius carved on a stone stele. Housed in the Shensi Provincial Museum, Xian, China.

Page 58 (bottom): The cave where Confucius was born, near Qufu, Shandong Province.

Page 59: A portion of a Tang dynasty (618–907) manuscript of the *Analects of Confucius*, unearthed in 1967 at Turfan, Sinkiang, China.

Page 60 (top): A c. fifteenth-century rendering of Laozi riding his ox, painted on silk with ink and watercolor. Housed in the National Palace Museum in Taipei, Taiwan.

Page 62: A seventeenth-century oil on panel portrait of Matteo Ricci, founder of the Jesuit mission in China. Housed in Gesu, Rome, Italy.

Page 64: The third century BC terra-cotta army of Emperor Qin Shihuangdi, discovered in 1974 near X'ian, China.

Page 66: A stretch of the Great Wall of China near Beijing. The wall began to be built during the Qin dynasty (221–202 BC).

Page 67 (top): A Neolithic era (6000–1500 BC) Chinese clay vase with swirl motif.

Page 67 (bottom): An elephant-shaped ritual vase c. 1500–1000 BC. Housed in the Musee des Arts Asiatiques-Guimet, Paris, France.

Page 68: An earthenware tomb brick, c. 206 BC–AD 9. Housed in the Museum of Fine Arts, Houston, Texas.

Page 69 (top): A c. 907–960 painting on silk, illustrating part of the Avatamsaka sutra. Housed in the Musee des Arts Asiatiques-Guimet, Paris, France.

Page 70: A painting from the late tenth or early eleventh century entitled *Snowy Landscape* by Fan Kuan.

Page 71 (top): A fourteenth-century ink on paper illustration entitled *Horse and Groom in Winter*, by Chao Meng-Fu. Housed in the National Palace Museum, Taipei, Taiwan.

Page 72: A large Ming dynasty (1368–1644) vase, made of china with enamel glaze. Housed in the Ashmolean Museum, Oxford, England.

Page 73: A nineteenth-century painting of Chinese silkmakers. Housed in the Free Library of Philadelphia, Philadelphia, Pennsylvania.

Page 78: A c. 1500 BC oracle bone. Housed in the British Museum, London, England.

Page 81: A mid-twelfth-century illustration to "The Ode of Chen." Housed in the British Museum, London, England.

Page 82 (top): An early twentieth-century photograph of Lu Xun.

Page 82 (bottom): The book jacket of a volume of Lu Xun's short stories entitled *Panghuang (Wandering)*, published in 1926 by the Beixin Book Company. Designed by Tao Yuanqing.

Page 83: A 1970 AFP photo of People's Liberation Army soldiers reading Mao Zedong's Little Red Book.

Page 98: A film still from the Hong Kong movie *Crouching Tiger, Hidden Dragon* (2000), directed by Ang Lee.

Page 103: An eighteenth-century print by Kim Hong-Do of a Confucian classroom. Housed in the National Museum, Seoul, South Korea.

Page 105: A c. 1900 photograph of Kang Yu Wei.

Page 106 (top): A 1966 Associated Press photograph of Red Guards in Peking, China.

Page 106 (bottom): A 1972 photograph by Wally McNamee of a female university student and Red Guard member in Beijing.

Page 113: A May 4, 1989, photograph by Peter Turnley of protesters gathered in Tian'anmen Square in Beijing, China.

INDEX

About the Author

Gillian Houghton is a freelance writer in New York City.

Designer: Geri Fletcher; **Cover Designer:** Tahara Anderson;
Editor: John Kemmerer; **Photo Researcher:** Fernanda Rocha